Cloud by Day, Fire by Night

Led by His Presence Into His Promise

by

Jeremy Friedman

Cloud by Day, Fire by Night

Led by His Presence Into His Promise

by

Jeremy Friedman

Lighthouse Family Ministries, Inc.
www.LighthouseFM.net

Cloud by Day, Fire by Night

Led By His Presence Into His Promise

Requests for bulk sales discounts, editorial permissions, or other information should be addressed to:

Scroll Publishers
PO Box 5847
Pinehurst, NC 28374
USA

ISBN 13 TP: 978-1-962808-30-9
ISBN 13 eBook: 978-1-962808-31-6

Cover Design by Darian Horner Design (www.darianhorner.com)
Image: stock.adobe.com #925560999

First Edition: March 2026

10 9 8 7 6 5 4 3 2 1 0

Printed in the United States of America

Table of Contents

Acknowledgements

This book is dedicated first and foremost to the Lord God Almighty, who was, is, and is to come. Without His saving grace and mercy, I would not be alive today to write this volume of revelatory encounters He has blessed me with.

I want to acknowledge my wife, Joelene, whose patient endurance and unwavering support have been a strength during difficult seasons, always encouraging me not to hold back. Her trust and support in my journey to follow how God is leading has made this journey possible.

I wish to honor my spiritual family worldwide, (you know who you are), my many brothers, sisters, mothers, and fathers in the faith who have helped me grow continually in my relationship with the Lord and in the gifts of the Spirit.

Lastly, I would like to acknowledge the pioneers and forerunners in the body of believers—prophets and apostles—who go against the grain, forsaking what is popular and allowing themselves to be guided by the unction of the Holy Spirit. Their walk can be lonely and sometimes even hard, but their unwavering ability to always choose the

Lord's way over their own, despite trials and challenges, is always a path to God's goodness. They take many metaphorical arrows to release revelation and reformation to the body, and for that example of dying to self and following Him no matter how it looks, I am truly grateful.

Foreword

It was an honor when Jeremy asked if I would write the foreword to his newest book, *Cloud by Day, Fire by Night*. Jeremy and his beautiful family came into my life about four years ago in an unusual way.

My family and I were just finishing the last touches on a very special place called The Safe House—an assignment from the Lord to create a place where people could come and encounter God. We had not yet held our first service when we were asked if a ministry could use our facility to host their conference. We said yes, although the chairs we had ordered months prior had still not arrived. The conference was still weeks away, but the day before their conference—still no chairs! It truly was a miracle after taking the matter of the delayed chairs into the Courts of Heaven. The next day we were notified they were found in North Carolina and were scheduled to be held for several more weeks. Needless to say, several men from The Safe House flew up, rented trucks, loaded them, and made a quick turnaround back to Florida. We were so thankful to the Lord and knew He had made a way where there seemed to be no way.

It was at this conference that Jeremy and his wife, Joelene, were in attendance, flying in from New York to Florida. There were several hundred people in attendance, but Jeremy and Joelene stood out to me by the Holy Spirit. I prayed with them several times during the altar services. It was during this conference that the Lord instructed them to move from New York to be a part of the assignment called The Safe House.

It wasn't long before his family of seven had moved and begun to settle in and flow with what God was beginning to build—a place so unique that the presence of the Lord was tangible, and services were totally His will.

Jeremy and Joelene were among the first to join our weekly intercession prayer meetings. It was a place of teaching on intercession and praying out the heart of God upon whatever was on His heart. During this time, Israel was attacked and war broke out. There were nights that we would come together under the leadership and direction of the Holy Spirit to intercede for Israel. It was during this season that I observed Jeremy becoming more alive and sensitive to the leading of the Holy Spirit. Jeremy had already learned and experienced entering into the Courts of Heaven prayer, but I was honored to witness his spiritual growth—to sit on the sidelines of his life and watch the journey that God wants to take all of us on. Yes, encountering Him and being taught by Heaven the mysteries and operations of Kingdom authority—not only in Heaven but also in what God wants on Earth.

This book that you hold in your hands will cause you to hunger and also to wonder, is this real? There are areas that, if you are still under the influence of religious teachings by man or demons, may cause you to shut the book and not read any more until the time of the Holy Spirit's cutting away of religious teachings and mindsets. And then one day, you will pick up where you left off and read on. Could this book possibly be the beginning of your own journey into Heavenly encounters—your own secret places of revelation—not only about Heaven and the cloud of witnesses, but also about your own life? A journey that always leads you to encounter *Him*, the Lord of Lords and the King of Kings, and into a relationship you never thought possible? I pray this will be so.

I once asked Jeremy why he wanted to share his encounters that are so personal to him, and his reply was, "I don't know why, but I do know the Father asked me to!" Oh, how wonderful are the workings of the Holy Spirit in each of our lives. To God be the Glory forevermore, who still leads us sometimes in strange ways. For Moses and the people of Israel, He was the cloud and the fire.

Jeremy and I join with the Apostle Paul, who prayed for those he loved in the first chapter of Ephesians, that all of our eyes would be opened, and that we and all of our families would have revelation, understanding, and wisdom to be able to comprehend the supernatural will of God.

YOU ARE THE BELOVED!

Gaila Carroll
Intercessor, Habitation Church
& Lover of the Holy Spirit
Estero, Florida

Preface

As I sat in the presence of the Lord, soaking on a Monday morning in late May of 2024, the cry of my heart was for the Lord to increase the fear of the Lord in my life and in my generations, and to send the "terror of Adonai" upon our enemies (2 Chronicles 14:13). As I meditated on this Scripture and on King Asa's revival lifestyle, I was taken into an encounter.

It was Memorial Day on Earth, but as I peered into the realm of the spirit in Heaven, I saw twelve piles of rocks, carefully stacked one upon the next. They were called memorial stones, and before the twelve piles stood many from the Cloud of Witnesses. As I walked toward the family of God, I saw far beyond the initial twelve—many more piles of memorial stones stretching into the distance.

A man came forth and began speaking to me; it was Moses. He welcomed me to this field, called the Field of Honor in Heaven. Moses explained that each of these pillars of stone was a tribute to the Father for His faithfulness, and each represented a memory of a victory in which God had provided a miraculous and triumphant outcome for one of His children.

As I listened to the sounds of Heaven, I heard the stones singing praises and honor to God. The frequency of their sound was soothing to my spirit, and the melodies carried beauty far beyond anything recognizable on Earth. These frequencies of praise opened a gateway of Heavenly light in the midst of the field.

As I watched eagerly to discover what lay beyond this radiant portal of pure white light, I saw Jesus standing there, inviting us to step through. The moment we crossed the threshold, we found ourselves in the magnificent throne room of Heaven. Before us stood the King of Glory, radiant with majesty, holding in His right hand a remarkable living element—something like the symbol of an atom or molecule.

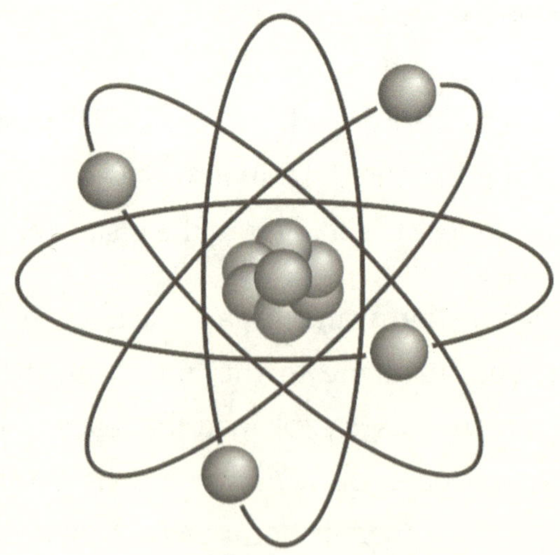

As I gazed at this living element He held, Jesus spoke, *"It's time for us to go back to the beginning."*

At His words, I chuckled inwardly, thinking that "the beginning" started with *Adam*—and in His hand was an *atom*. No sooner had He spoken than all I could see was darkness; all before me was void. Like thunder, I heard a voice speak unrecognizable words, but my spirit knew it meant "let there be light" and "Tov" (the Hebrew word for *"good"*).

As I watched the narrative of creation unfold, it was like watching a movie; more glorious and spectacular than one could imagine or describe. I could sense the goodness of God and the fullness of His love in every nuance of created life. The energy within the air felt pure, even holy. But suddenly, there was a war: it was between holiness and sin, and the first Adam and his beloved Eve caved to the pressures and enticements of the flesh. Time seemed to speed up, and in what seemed like a flash, centuries played out in mere seconds, like a time-lapsed video.

As the playback stopped, I saw myself standing among thousands of people; they were the children of Israel. Moses was leading them from captivity through the wilderness. This was the period of wandering, but there wasn't just a physical wandering; it was the wandering of hearts and minds; they were straying from God. In the midst of this vision, I saw the words *course correction* and the numbers 9:19.

As I looked for a corresponding scripture in the Word, what I stumbled upon was the key I needed to understand this encounter.

> *Yet in Your manifold mercies You did not forsake them in the wilderness. The pillar of the cloud did not depart from them by day to lead them on the road, nor the pillar of fire by night, to show them light and the way they should go.* (Nehemiah 9:19)

As I came out of this encounter, I knew this was a season of being led by the Spirit of God. The world has become our wilderness and place of wandering, but it was time to turn back to Him, to retake our rightful place at His right hand and walk in the promised power of the Holy Spirit—to save the lost, preach the Gospel, heal the sick, and cast out devils. The only way for the bride to get back to her first love was to follow the cloud by day and the pillar of fire by night. I pray that this volume does exactly that.

I pray that the revelation within these pages provokes something deep within you—a cry to know Him more, a hunger and thirst to do what He has done, to love Him and be lovesick for Jesus. I pray these words are sweet in your heart but a fire in your soul, burning away the remnants of religion and purifying your heart to stand before Him blameless and holy, for the Spirit of righteousness dwells within you. Today is your day to rise as a son and to walk in full access and authority to all that Heaven has prepared for you. I bless you to be free to step into this from this day forward, in Jesus' name. Amen.

Chapter 1
Dimensional Shifts

The heart of the Father is for all of His children to learn to yield to the sound of His voice—to hear Him, to know Him, and to encounter Him. As we choose to put aside the things that distract us from the presence of God, we begin cultivating habits of relational intimacy that open doors to revelation far beyond our imagination. These are the wisdoms of Heaven, and from this place we receive truth, knowledge, divine ideas, and strategies for life. The Father longs to release these encounters to us. Such revelation can transform us, deliver us, heal us, and elevate our understanding of the world around us.

One summer morning, such an encounter took place—one that challenged many paradigms I had held for years. I was driving down Alligator Alley between Naples and Miami, watching the sun rise in the east. Its beauty stirred worship in my heart as I praised God for His marvelous works. As I prayed, the voice of the Holy Spirit interrupted me, and what He had to say was simply perspective changing.

He began speaking to me about dimensional realities and how these shifts affect the three-dimensional Earth. Heaven explained that as the Earth has shifted dimensionally, we have witnessed changes on the planet. One example was the increasingly vivid colors seen at sunrise and sunset over the past decade. Heaven said these changes are the result of the Earth physically translating into another dimension as it moves through space and time.

As I pondered this, I suddenly gained insight into many phenomena, what some call the Mandela Effect, societal shifts, sudden changes in governmental structures, increasing darkness, and even changes in weather patterns.

I understood that as these dimensional shifts occurred, warfare intensified. Evil attempted to overtake the planet, and humanity, especially the Church—did not fully comprehend what was happening. I began to grasp how these things worked in tandem, and as I heard them in the Spirit, I was prompted to search the internet for the concept of a fifth dimension. I saw results for "fifth-dimensional Earth" on Google and discovered that this is an actual scientific theory of quantum physics in existence.

The Holy Spirit said that this is a period of awakening and enlightenment for all the Earth, but especially for the sons of God to come up higher and into a greater understanding of their destiny, their identity, and their ability to co-create with

Father to rule and reign as governing sons and to judge wickedness from heavenly places.

In that moment I understood that when Scripture speaks of the new heavens, the new Earth, and the New Jerusalem, it may describe the physical Earth shifting dimensionally—merging with heavenly realms until Heaven and Earth become one. The collision of these realms will produce the new creation foretold in prophecy.

As I began to receive this revelation, I realized that this idea was not so far-fetched. As Heaven spoke to me about this, I was driving on the highway at sunrise and noticed that I could see every color of the rainbow. That was when the revelation faucet was fully turned on. I started to realize that in recent years, both at sunrise and sunset, I had seen other colors of the spectrum that I didn't recall being present decades earlier. I noticed purples and greens that I didn't remember seeing in my youth. Not only did I not recall seeing them, but as I searched for historic photos of sunrises and sunsets, the results led me to the conclusion that these colors had not been there. Additionally, I realized that there were shadows and other representations that had only begun to appear in the imagery taken in more recent years.

This was all way too complex for me to comprehend, and in surrender, all I could speak out was, "Your ways are not our ways, Lord, but all of your paths are peace, and may your peace be upon us."

As I stared into the sunrise, I could see individual rays shooting over the horizon, beautiful orange and white rays spanning across the indigo, blue, and purple parts of the sky. It was simply heavenly, and I wondered at what point in time things shifted so that we could behold this new dimension of beauty.

As I continued to wrestle with this topic and seek Heaven's truth above the new-age and scientific versions of it, I asked the Father for more clarity. The Father explained that the new-age philosophies are demonically forged versions of kingdom truth, and with implications that hurt and imprison others. They do not have the lasting change and impact that kingdom truth does.

The Holy Spirit said, *"Let me ask you a question... when you got baptized, gave your life to Jesus, and were filled with the Holy Spirit, did you experience a change in the way you think, act, and speak?"*

I replied, "Yes, I was transformed." He explained that this is evidence of a dimensional shift; it can also be seen as a way our paradigms and thought processes can shift and evolve.

The new-age concept of ascension and its philosophies are lies and traps that copy what happens when one actually gives their life to the Lord and becomes filled with the Holy Spirit. The only way into true enlightenment, truth, and magnificent change is through a relationship with Jesus.

As an example of this, I was led to a vision of Jesus on the Mount of Transfiguration, transforming and revealing Himself as the glorified Son of God. This was a shift of dimensional energy from the place where Earth resided into a higher plane or dimension: the heavenly realm. He explained that when we step into Heaven in the spirit, we experience these types of shifts even though our physical bodies are still in the natural realm.

Wisdom's Pearl

One Sunday morning, while worshiping, I felt unrest in my soul. Though the week had been blessed, I sensed the enemy attempting to stir attitudes and emotions in my home. As I sought Heaven, I was suddenly taken into a vision.

Moses and Enoch appeared before me in a crystalline hallway in Heaven. Moses extended his hand and placed a pearl in mine. "This is a pearl of wisdom."

As I examined it, Enoch said, "Do not forget—the battles belong to the Lord."

Instantly, the scenery changed. I was in the middle of a war zone. Angels clashed with principalities. Demons fled before hosts of Heaven. In the midst of this battlefield stood a dome of glass-like light surrounding me, my family, and the men in white.

Inside the dome stood a woman of radiant white light, shimmering like diamonds, with golden hair and blue eyes. This was Wisdom, the personality of the Holy Spirit.

Wisdom spoke, "When you stand in peace, you are within the Citadel of the Lord. Nothing can shake your foundation. Often the best response to small fires is no response at all. Keep your gaze upon Jesus. Give no attention to the schemes of hell. Many fires extinguish themselves when ignored."

She continued, "Stand armored. Stay fastened to the gospel of peace. He is your foundation."

As she spoke, the battlefield cleared. Darkness fled. The dome dissolved. The war zone transformed into a vibrant garden.

Moses said, "It is peace."

Returning to myself, I saw my natural surroundings calming in the same way—on Earth as it is in Heaven.

Wisdom then said, "True wisdom is knowing when to keep silent, when to engage Heaven, and when not to engage from the soul-ruled realm. Everything must bow to Jesus. Stay spirit-first. Pray in the Spirit on all occasions—for this is the way."

Holy Ground

After this, I was shown a vision of Moses atop Mount Sinai receiving the 10 Commandments. From the mountaintop, I could see the full moon casting its beautiful light over the valley below. As I entered this vision, I heard a voice say, *"Remove your shoes from your feet, for the place on which you stand is holy ground."*

Revelation came quickly—I understood that our hearts and minds are holy ground. When we allow lies, cultural norms, or worldly belief systems to take root, we pollute what belongs to Him.

> *Have you forgotten that your body is now the sacred temple of the Spirit of Holiness, who lives in you? You don't belong to yourself any longer, for the gift of God, the Holy Spirit, lives inside your sanctuary. You were God's expensive purchase, paid for with tears of blood, so by all means, then, use your body to bring glory to God!* (1 Corinthians 6:19-20, TPT)

Compromise not only destroys our calling, but wrong belief systems also weaken our faith and expectation to see God move. Allowing what is defiling and contrary to the Word of God to remain will make us impotent and powerless as sons unless we are careful to adhere only to the righteousness of God, which was purchased for us on the cross. We must not be a generation fearful to stand against what is wrong. We cannot tolerate Jezebel in our churches and communities; we must cast out the impostor and the candy-coated gospel. We must rise up and be table-flipping sons in the face of deception, as Jesus was.

> *Upon entering Jerusalem, Jesus went directly into the temple area and drove out all the merchants who were buying and selling their goods. He overturned the tables of the money changers and the stands of those selling doves. He said to them, 'My dwelling place will be known as a house of prayer, but you have made it into a hangout for thieves!'* (Matthew 21:12-13, TPT)

If we sincerely want to walk as our Savior did, we must lay down our lives, take up our cross, and walk unashamedly, on fire for all God has placed within us. We must embrace pruning and crushing, and rejoice in persecutions, knowing that the outcome of trials and tests will be righteousness that allows God's glory to rest on us and flow through us.

Building the Altar of the Lord

As I sought the Lord further, He said, *"My son, many religious people have entered Heaven because their faith in My Son united them with eternal life—even though they did not understand sonship. But many who treat church as a club, without love for God, will not enter in.*

"The altar of the Lord must be established in a man's personal life, in his home, and in his family. This altar is a threshing floor and dwelling place of My presence. Oil flows into those who build the altar—oil they are meant to pour out upon others. But many come to the house of the Lord empty, seeking only to be filled, rather than coming filled to worship."

Transition Time

As I continued to listen, pausing in the presence of the Lord to hear what He had to say, I heard the words *Transition Time.* Before me in the Spirit stood a whirlwind, and as I looked around, I saw another behind me, one to my left, and a fourth to my right. These were the four winds: one from the north, one from the south, one from the east, and finally the west wind. As I watched them spin, I heard the Holy Spirit say these winds bring change, ushering in new seasons and marking the end of others.

"You are entering a new season, one not of trial but of testing. A release is coming from the Father, but as it is in transit, the times of testing have intensified; this season will leave many weary, yet you, beloved child, have been chosen. The Father has determined that you are worthy to endure

such testing at this time. As this season concludes, you will be put in charge of much if you remain faithful until the end."

I saw Phillip, my personal angel, standing nearby, holding a spear in a determined and ready stance. I heard the Spirit of the Lord say, *"Stand firm, hold your peace, hold your ground, and above all, restrain your tongue from the grumbles and complaints of murmuring. You are more than qualified to undertake all I have entrusted to you. Be still, receive wisdom, and flow in the grace of the gifts you possess. The Father is pleased with your dedication and determination, and now it's time to go west, to seek Him and find Him!"*

As I turned to the Word after this encounter, I was stunned to see the confirmation in the books of Daniel and Mark, revealing just how near the Father is to those who seek Him. I was brought to the following verses of scripture to add credence to this encounter. Daniel said:

> *I saw in my vision by night, and behold, the four winds of Heaven were stirring up the great sea (the nations).* (Daniel 7:2, AMP)

> *And then He will send out the angels and will gather together His elect [those He has chosen for Himself] from the four winds, from the farthest end of the Earth to the farthest end of Heaven.* (Mark 13:27, AMP)

Chapter 2
Prophetic Intercession

As I was deep in intercession one afternoon, I was greeted by several men in white linen. My spirit recognized them immediately: E. M. Bounds, Daniel Nash, and Charles Finney.

I heard Heaven say, "In your past season, many of the prophets in the Cloud of Witnesses have been trading into your life. Although they continue to do so, these are some of the intercessors trading into you in this season. A prophet's most powerful gift is intercession, and an intercessor's most powerful key is the prophetic; they go hand in hand. Intercessors are the watchmen on the wall who prepare the way; prophets are the gatekeepers who shut down hell and usher forth Heaven. Together, these gifts operate in unity and inflict serious damage to the enemy's plans."

As I heard this, the lightning of God surged through me, and I felt the frequency of Heaven radiating across my physical body. I shook under the power of the Holy Spirit.

I saw the Word of God appear before me, opening to a specific passage—Jeremiah 21. In the midst of the book burned a flame of fire that did not consume the pages. It was the flame of the intercessor's heart—the flame that breaks through opposition, the flame that ignites the Father's heart in agreement with the very things Jesus intercedes for at this moment before the throne.

By faith, I received this impartation and asked the Father to activate my calling as a prophetic intercessor.

Intercessors Posture

Another morning, the Spirit of God said, *"You are in the middle of a massive test."*

As I looked in the Spirit, I saw myself kneeling. Radiant white light surrounded me, while overhead swirled charcoal-gray clouds. In the atmosphere above, the clouds took the form of dragon-like heads—three of them—watching from above as though waiting to strike. Yet the light held them back.

As I prayed in tongues, I heard the Holy Spirit explain that these forces had come to strike my heart, my mind, my foundation, my work, my family, and my ministry. Suddenly, they lunged toward me. In the Spirit, I rose with a sword of brilliant light and severed the three heads in a single stroke.

I watched myself return to the kneeling posture—unmoved, unshaken, unhindered. The atmosphere cleared, and I continued praying.

Then I heard, *"Posture yourself in intercession, and nothing shall by any means make you afraid."*

Watchtower

On another afternoon, I heard Heaven say it was time to build the *watchtower.* When I asked what this meant, I was shown that it represented watchful prayer over the wavering hearts of believers in every nation—those called to intercede during times of war in Heaven and on earth.

Heaven said, "Some will be awakened at midnight. Others will feel restlessness in their spirit as new strategies and the Father's words burst forth like water from a dam. The flow of Heaven will increase for those answering this call to be watchmen on the wall. They will shake and weep in travail before the Lord. The journey will be long and difficult, but the rewards and the fruit will be unlike anything seen before."

We are entering the final phase—the beginning of the end of the age. Times are changing quickly; days feel shorter and hours pass swiftly. Many hearts are failing because of fear. Remain watchful. Stay in faith. It is your shield and buckler.

The Walk of the Intercessor

The next morning, as I stepped into Heaven, it felt as though I stood on the shore of a beach with storm-like clouds forming in the distance. The waters were rough and choppy. As I inquired about the scene, a warm breeze blew across me. As it strengthened, I heard, *"This is the walk of an intercessor."*

Understanding came instantly. Those who stand in the gap on earth draw the full attention of the enemy. Hell focuses its strategies, minions, and assaults against the intercessor. The Lord entrusts us with the resistance—to refuse the temptation to lay down our swords, to abandon the mantle, or to turn away from the high calling released upon our lives. We are called to bring change to the earth, disrupt the adversary's schemes, and tear down the gates of hell through prayer.

Then I heard the Spirit of the Lord, *"The gates of hell must not prevail in this hour. My son, turmoil and turbulence are escalating on earth. The pressure My intercessors have faced has been monumental, and it will intensify—yet strengthen your heart. Strengthen the hearts of those around you. Lift up their arms, and let them lift yours, that all may be empowered in these final days. The onslaught against My intercessors is increasing as wickedness grows; but do not fear. Breakthrough is at hand. Relief is on the way. The armies of Heaven have been dispatched with new strategies, tools, and weaponry that will make a dramatic difference."*

In the Spirit, I saw rockets launching from the very words that came out of my mouth. They fired into the turbulent waters, erupting in mushroom clouds of smoke and mist. As this happened, the storm clouds dissolved. The distant waters calmed. Sunlight broke forth over the sea. Stillness replaced the wind, and peace settled over everything.

Then I heard: *"This is the fruit of intercession. This is what comes after the burden is lifted—after the shaking in the Spirit is released through the power of your words. Let your tongues roar like a lion over the earth, over the nations, and over the jurisdiction I am granting you in this hour. Call forth what is to come. Stand against what is not meant to overtake the children of God."*

Chapter 3
Throne Room Intercession

As I engaged with Heaven on the afternoon of July 12th, 2024, I was taken into a vision where I found myself among many who were gathered in the Throne Room. My soul was overwhelmed—thoughts, emotions, and burdens pressed heavily—while my spirit wrestled to see and hear what the Holy Spirit was witnessing before the Throne. As peace slowly settled within me, I saw angels of revelation along with angels assigned to various earthly structures. Each had been designated by the Father to assist the saints—and in this moment, to assist me—in stewarding different assignments.

I fell to my knees and postured my heart in worship before the Father's throne. In the Throne Room, I saw a giant bowl of incense burning—prayers of the saints rising as a fragrant offering before His nostrils. But to my surprise, the flames on this altar appeared diminished. The smoke did not rise in its usual abundance; instead, the plume was faint and thin.

From deep within me, a cry burst forth—an anguished wail across Heaven—calling for the angels to go forth and awaken the intercessors in this hour, to rouse the Bride from her slumber. A fog of witchcraft and darkness had descended upon the Earth, placing her in a sleep not easily shaken.

From Heaven, I saw strategies of distraction and division taking hold. Intercessors and the sons of God had been subtly lulled into sleep through frequencies broadcast by television, media, and news streams—frequencies of gossip, conspiracy, and rumor. These influences had begun infiltrating the body, and the hearts of the burning ones grew cold. As I beheld this, I wept and cried out, "Forgive us, for we know not what we do."

An angel named *Revelation* appeared before me and handed me a scroll. I heard the Father and Jesus, speaking out to all of Heaven saying, *"Who will stand in the gap for the intercessors that have grown weary and burdened in their assignments? Who will be as a Daniel in this hour? Who will take the sins of the bride upon themselves and bring them before me in my courts, that they may be purged and removed. That freedom may come this hour?"* (see Daniel 9:1-19)

All of Heaven began to wail. Cries of the saints resounded before God's throne. In unison, Heaven interceded for vindication and strengthening. I stared downward through the sea of glass like crystal, the very floor of the Throne

Room—and saw the whole Earth and all creation. (see Revelation 4, 5)

Across the Earth, I saw vipers moving stealthily among the people of God. They multiplied in the ears of the saints, and when they locked eyes with them, the serpents' gaze began to swirl—hypnotizing those who once burned brightly. In a trance, their gaze shifted from the throne of God toward drunkenness, lust, immorality, perversion, selfish desire, and murderous intent. Their motives were polluted—compromise had seared the conscience of many, and the line between holy and profane had faded from view.

Heaven continued to weep, and then Jesus cried out, *"Is there none who will stand in the gap in this hour? Is there none who will stand for the redemption of a generation becoming crooked and twisted? Is there none geared in the full armor of God—ready to unleash the forces of Heaven upon the Earth?"*

The Celestial Court and the Scroll of Repentance

By faith, I received the scroll of revelation and spoke from the depths of my spirit, "Jesus, we shall stand in this hour. Will You take us into Your courts?"

The moment the words left my mouth, we were instantly transported into the Celestial Court of Heaven—the highest of the courts. (Daniel 7:9–14)

A weighty holiness permeated the atmosphere. The heavy glory of the Lord filled the chamber as we stood before the Ancient of Days. The courtroom radiated light, judgment, mercy, and timeless authority.

Before Him, the accusations and legal rights of the enemy against the body of Christ were presented. I stepped forward and declared:

"Ancient of Days, I come before You in the name of Jesus. I agree with the accuser of the brethren in every area where Your people have opened the door. I repent on behalf of the saints and our generations for where we have profaned the calling of God upon our lives. We repent for the lust of the flesh, the lust of the eyes, and the pride of life. We repent for gossip, slander, and hypocrisy. We repent for partnering with the lies of the adversary, spreading rumors, and allowing ourselves to be hypnotized and overtaken by collusion in our hearts and minds. We repent for where blessings were stolen because of unholy agreements. We repent of debauchery, murderous intent, idolatry, wrong motives, and the selfishness we embraced. We repent for entertaining witchcraft, and for honoring those who operated in control and manipulation over the presence of the living God. We repent for the wolves in sheep's clothing who caused many to fall away, and we confess all of this as sin. I ask that the blood of Jesus be applied—from the Father's hands back through every place it must go—washing every legal right and every impact in Jesus' name."

As I waited for the verdict, angels shifted into position around the courtroom. Authority rose within me, and I declared:

"In Jesus' name, I loose these angels to go in time and out of time—in every timeline, age, realm, and dimension—to remove every power, principality, throne, dominion, demon, spirit, or familiar spirit operating in the lives of the intercessors and the sons of God. Remove them to the abyss in Jesus' name."

The angels went forth, and I saw serpents being pulled away from the saints. One by one, the sons of God awakened from their hypnotized state. As they came to themselves, they fell prostrate before the Father—both in Heaven and on the Earth. Worship rose in unified waves.

Then I saw altars highlighted throughout the world—in the second heavens, and even beneath the seas. Angels were commanded to gather these altars along with their attendants and bring them into the courtroom for judgment.

As the angels brought them in, I saw witches, warlocks, and practitioners of sorcery whose spirits had accessed the spiritual realm illegally through occult means such as astral travel (see 1 Corinthians 6:3–4).

There were marine and water spirits, incubus and succubus spirits, marriage-breaking spirits, spirits of fear and suicide, pride and rebellion, python, Jezebel, Ahab, Lilith, Dagon, Baphomet, and Satan himself.

As I stood and watched, I cried out:

"Father, I repent on behalf of the Saints and all who walked in these occult practices. We repent for embracing marine and water spirits, incubus and succubus, marriage-breaking spirits, fear, suicide, pride, rebellion, python, Jezebel, Ahab, Lilith, Dagon, Baphomet, and Satan. We confess these as sin. I ask that the blood of Jesus cancel, void, and nullify every legal right, impact, and assignment of each one presented here. I ask for the utter destruction of every profane and ungodly altar and its attendants. I ask that they be gathered and sent immediately to the abyss of Revelation 20:3, never to return. I ask the angels to cut the silver cords and crush the golden bowls of all who attempt to astrally project into the realms of the people of God. (Ecclesiastes 12:6–7) I request a permanent spiritual restraining order from the Court of Enforcement—that nothing and no one may take their place in these assignments." (Ezekiel 13:17–23)

The Ancient of Days slammed His gavel. "It is finished."

At His decree, angels rounded up every entity and removed them. As the verdict echoed through the court, all the angels cried out,

Holy is the Lord God! Holy is the Lamb! (Revelation 4-5)

I interceded again, "Lord, send the angels to rebuild the altars of the Lord—the family altars, the personal altars, the godly altars—where our sacrifice of praise and worship rises before You as a pleasing aroma."

Suddenly, we were back in the throne room. I saw the fire of intercession burning like a blazing inferno. Plumes of incense—prayers of the saints—rose in thick, fragrant waves, filling Heaven with a sweet smell like frankincense and vanilla.

Crying Out Before the Throne

As I looked into Heaven another morning, I found myself before the Throne of the Lord. Before Him, many *Saints* were gathered, weeping and wailing, crying out, "How much longer until You avenge Your people? How much longer until the time of the return?"

Prayers were rising from the Earth into the Throne Room—intermingling with the prayers of the Saints in Heaven—and all came up before the Father like incense. I heard Heaven say, "Just a little while longer until the number of those martyred for their faith is complete."

The weeping in Heaven over the innocent blood shed upon the Holy Land was overwhelming. As I beheld it, I myself began to weep. A phrase echoed repeatedly in my spirit, *"Pray for the peace of Jerusalem."*

When I looked down upon the Earth through the floor of the Throne Room, I saw the words *wars and rumors of wars* burning like fire across strategic regions. Principalities had been permitted to stir up war in certain places.

Then I heard, *"Idolatry will be brought low. Prepare My Bride, and tell her the days of My coming are quickly approaching. Now is the time, and now is the season to prepare your dwelling places—to return to what is eternal and refuse what is fleeting and fading away."*

I asked, "Are You bringing judgment upon Your people, Lord?"

He answered, *"No. I am bringing redemption."*

I asked, "How are we to pray?"

The Lord responded, *"Pray for deliverance from their oppressors and captors. Loose the armies of Heaven to uproot every hidden cabal aligned against the people of Israel. Pray for those on the Earth—for the tribes of the Gentile nations—that their hearts be softened and turned toward Israel. Pray for restoration and unity, that the brethren may dwell together in peace. Pray for Israel and the Jewish people to come to know the path of redemption, that all may be saved and none perish. Pray that the generations—and younger generations—grow up with love and adoration for My people and for Jerusalem, knowing the value of her treasure and the portion of their inheritance in the Holy Land and among My people."*

Receiving Revelation

During the COVID era, I had a profound encounter with Heaven that involved receiving revelations for ministries and guidance on how to pray them through. I was still new to my daily interactions with Heaven, learning to break free from religion and follow the Holy Spirit. As I ventured into the heavenly realms on this particular day, I was taken into an engagement with the *Cloud of Witnesses*. I stood in a place that felt like the center of the universe—galaxies swirling above, below, and around me—yet I could walk on solid ground. The church in Heaven seemed pleased and eagerly anticipating my arrival.

I was shown how the Lord had endowed me with unique gifts in the arts—particularly visual art and music—and how other gifts in my life would emerge in future seasons.

Two men in white linen approached to guide me; their names were Michael and Angelo. I chuckled inwardly—God clearly had a sense of humor, especially since I was an art major. *Michelangelo* was an unmistakable nod.

Michael and Angelo showed me how my artistic skills were being used for the Lord in the three ministries I served on Earth. Looking with them at the Earth from outside of time, I saw strands of light wrapping around the globe through LifeSpring International Ministries. For Shuvah Yisrael Messianic Synagogue, bluish strands of light struck regions across the United States, Israel, the Middle East, Europe, New Zealand, and Iceland. Michael and Angelo even highlighted Reykjavik, Iceland, noting a small but growing Messianic Jewish population that would expand in coming years.

For the Nazarene Church, I saw a Godly fire spreading through denominational Christianity—once present in only a handful of churches—igniting a Spirit-filled revival that removed long-standing obstacles hindering spiritual growth.

Then they handed me a key and a sealed scroll. The key unlocked the scroll, which unrolled into an exceptionally long document. It spoke of my work, my business, and my future, reassuring me that the Lord was pouring out blessing and provision and encouraging me to keep moving forward.

Later, during another encounter, the *Cloud of Witnesses* visited us during prayer time. They sat at a table with my wife, Joelene, and me. Many Saints brought gifts for specific purposes. King David handed Joelene a scroll of administration for rest. Jesus gave us understanding to know and pray the Father's heart. James brought a scroll concerning the wise use of our tongues—to bless and not to curse. John the Baptist presented a scroll of preparation.

The Holy Spirit spoke to Joelene, saying, *"Come out of your cocoon, spread your wings, and fly. This is a season for your spiritual growth and development; do everything for the Lord, not for people."*

Jesus then rose and became the glorious Lord, shining brightly like diamonds in white light. Then Job and Moses appeared, standing behind and beside me. Job handed me the scroll of walking in integrity. Moses gave Joelene the scroll of leadership for guiding as a mother to nations, a confidant to widows, and a sister to those who are lost broken.

The Strategy Room

At another time, as I entered the secret place, I found myself walking into a vast room that resembled an old museum. Golden and white marble floors echoed softly beneath my feet. Along both walls, glass cases displayed artifacts, maps, weapons, and items from many generations.

Ahead of me was a long table surrounded by men and women. As I passed the final display case, a single word dropped into my spirit: *Saigon.* It felt reminiscent of the fall of Saigon that ended the Vietnam War.

Approaching the table, I saw many gathered, with Jesus seated at the center. A large map lay spread before them, marked with strategic pieces reminiscent of the board game *Stratego.* Bookshelves lined the outer walls—volumes on war strategy, business strategy, intercession, ministry, family planning, wealth building, farming, and more.

Those gathered around the table were receiving intercessory assignments and strategies for their respective roles and the areas they were charged with interceding for. Each person was given a small scroll, tied shut with a ribbon, meant only for that person's eyes.

A man approached and handed me one of the scrolls. My spirit recognized him as Jehu—one of the Saints in Heaven, a military commander in the Lord's army. He pressed the scroll to my chest and said, "Use wisdom. This gift is dangerous in the wrong hands, and its weight is crushing in the right hands."

As I looked at the scroll, the outside bore the inscription "Proverbs 3:5-6."

Trust in the Lord with all your heart, And lean not on your own understanding; In all your ways acknowledge Him, And He shall direct your paths. (Proverbs 3:5-6)

When I opened the scroll, I found only three words inside—*NEVER GIVE UP.*

As I read this, a blue wave of electricity came out of the parchment and spread throughout my arms, legs, and body.

I heard Heaven say, "This is the fortitude of the Father and the gift of perseverance. Though the war is intense and the opposition immense, you shall overcome. Don't give up!"

Then I sensed Heaven add, "Intercession is most effective when your spirit is broken and your heart contrite. Let anguish and oppression propel you into the Father's arms and become the catalyst for unwavering faith."

The Father spoke, *"My son, be still. Stop striving to force things; allow them to unfold in their time. The place I am taking you is unlike anything you've experienced. Your prophetic accuracy will increase, and your perception and discernment will surpass previous seasons. You will see in both the natural and spiritual realms. You are standing on the brink of a massive breakthrough and a geographic shift of seismic proportions.*

"Growth brings crushing, pressing, and the stripping away of what no longer serves you. Are you willing?"

I responded, "Yes—yes, Lord. I am willing, whatever the cost."

The Father continued, *"The enemy anticipates your breakthrough, which is why you have been burdened with familiar spirits and memories of old wounds. Look beyond the fog of illusion. See past the desires of the world and the flesh, and move toward your high calling in the Messiah. You are the Melchizedek of your household. This is your season of breakthrough."*

As He spoke, I saw the angel named Breakthrough standing nearby, holding a sledgehammer and tapping it eagerly against his palm.

Later that morning, I saw scrolls of destiny unfurling down a mountain. Many formed pathways, and those I had prayed for walked upward along them—ascending the mountain of God on the scrolls of their destiny. I understood this image as essential for the Summit RCM logo, representing people climbing the mountain of God along their ordained paths.

I saw Gloria—a woman in white—holding two scrolls or books for me to write that morning. It resonated with what the Lord told me the week before about Lifespring Publishing and writing through that resource.

The Scroll of Revelatory Fire

On the night of December 6, 2023, as I prepared for bed, my personal angel, Phillip, appeared holding a fiery blue scroll. When I asked its meaning, he said it was a scroll of revelation—released from the Father to impart heavenly understanding to the Saints on Earth. These scrolls enable individuals to grasp insight far beyond natural limits.

Phillip continued, "This scroll is for your assignments in this season. Receive it into your heart."

By faith, I reached out my hand to take it.

Phillip added, "This scroll was crafted by the scribes of Heaven to give you insight for the writings you will publish this season. As you present yourself before Heaven, your vision and journaling will increase. This scroll is essential for the depth of revelation the Father is releasing to you. Rest often—your spirit receives far more in rest than when your soul is striving. When you do not enter rest, your soul blocks your spirit's engagement with Heaven."

As he spoke, I reclined on my couch and breathed deeply. My spiritual vision sharpened instantly. I saw Enoch nearby and other Saints of Heaven engaged in their duties. Children, animals, and countless others moved freely—aloof and carefree, with no worry or pain. Harmony filled the atmosphere.

As I absorbed this peace, I felt convicted for allowing my soul to become overwhelmed. The Father spoke, *"My child, do not fear. This is your learning path, and what you gain now will birth greater peace. This is a deeper revelation of maintaining peace and yielding to My Spirit. What you have endured is simply a trial, for you are an overcomer. Walk in triumph and victory. Enjoy the space you have been granted. When stress rises, return here instead of spiraling, and receive the revelatory flow from Heaven."*

I looked down and saw that the blue flames of the scroll had engulfed my entire body. Within the flames, I saw patterns, codes, and data—information being imparted for future use in writing and cataloging all the Father would ask of me.

Chapter 4
Assignments of the Lord

As I sat before the Lord, soaking in His presence one Sunday morning in the autumn of 2023, I saw that He had given me a book titled *Assignments of the Lord*. Suddenly, two mountains appeared before me with a river flowing between them. I heard the words *Kidron Valley*.

Wanting to understand the meaning, I looked it up. The Kidron is believed to be the valley mentioned in Joel 3:2–12, where God declares He will gather all nations in the Valley of Jehoshaphat for final judgment. In the New Testament, Jesus left the Last Supper with His disciples and crossed the Kidron Valley on His way to the Mount of Olives. It is the valley that separates the Temple Mount from the Mount of Olives.

I then heard the word *intifada*, meaning "shaking off," referring to the Palestinian uprisings beginning in 1987. Behind this word, I saw an end-times army of dark forces that worshiped the demonic principality Allah—the moon-god of ancient Mesopotamia. From this, I gained understanding that my intercessory assignment was to pray for Israel. After completing that assignment, I sought the Lord for the next steps.

Tearing Down Egypt

I was taken into another vision where Jesus showed me what looked like ancient Egypt during the days of Moses. I heard the Holy Spirit say that Egypt represented the influence behind the modern identity war and the agenda of the perverse entity fueling today's "woke" ideology. He revealed that this idolatry and wickedness stemmed from defilement that had lingered on the Earth since the days of Pharaoh.

I then saw a box placed in front of me. Jesus reached into it and pulled out a needle and thread. I heard the Holy Spirit speak, *"I am stitching together all kinds of things to weave and work for the good of My people. What seems like the evil of today is actually a turning point for My anointed. The war against flesh, violence, and debauchery on the Earth and in the USA is being won. The former things of defilement are passing away, giving rise to a generation that will hunger and thirst for righteousness.*

"Evil has been exposed and will continue to be revealed. The skirts of the wicked will be lifted, exposing their wrongdoing and indiscretions. Their credibility and plans

will be extinguished. Those called by My name will reap the rewards of righteousness as wickedness is brought to justice."

Light in the Darkness

As I continued seeking the Lord regarding these matters, I had a vision of walking with Him through a graveyard at midnight. A full moon shone overhead, and I sensed it was Halloween night. Through my own eyes, I saw the light of the Lord and the fire of God radiating outward from within me—beams of glory piercing the heavy darkness.

In the middle of the graveyard, I saw a circle of people practicing witchcraft as if holding a séance, a Ouija board between them. The number *4* flickered in candlelight. I felt Jesus overlaying me—almost as if I were wearing Him—and an orb of light, frequency, and glory expanded outward.

As the light increased, the darkness vanished. The grass beneath my feet turned vibrant green. The sky brightened into a radiant blue with white clouds drifting overhead. A rainbow arched across the heavens. Life burst forth—animals, children, people, and wildflowers.

I heard the Spirit whisper the Scripture:

The light shines in the darkness, and the darkness shall not overpower it. (John 1:5)

Then the Father spoke, *"My son, much opposition lies ahead. Do not let the pressure overcome you. Turn to Me for protection from the storm. I will give you rest when you are weary; I will be your strength when you cannot continue. I will be the wind at your back and the arrow at your feet. Turn to Me."*

The Lord then showed me how ministry leaders can fall into pride, stirring division that tears apart ministry families. He cautioned me, *"You were chosen and called to where you are now. This is My grace for you."*

Rebellious Nation and the Walk of the Righteous

At another time, as I entered the realm of the spirit, I asked the Lord how His prophets of old handled societal rebellion. Heaven encouraged me to seek insight from the prophets themselves. I was brought into a place governed by men and women in white, where I was greeted by Jeremiah the prophet. As he approached, I sensed a unity and kinship in the spirit.

He spoke, "There is a kinship among us."

I asked him, "How did you respond when people celebrated evil while you called them back to righteousness?"

He replied, "Often the words of the prophets are not heeded. You will be cursed, spat upon, and beaten for taking a righteous stand for the things of God. In my day, I was imprisoned and abused for obeying Him. Society has not changed. Things have become most abominable, yet God has a plan, and all this is part of the great redemption soon to come.

"Do not lose heart in speaking against wickedness. Even though people around you engage in worthless things, remain uncompromised. Focus on the things above and encourage them to return to their Heavenly Father and His Christ."

Spirit of Division

As that encounter ended, the Holy Spirit warned me that rebellion is intertwined with the spirit of division. He said this spirit has been active for a long time and continues to wreak havoc by dividing the body of Christ and destabilizing nations.

He explained, *"In this season, it seeks to divide governments, nations, and the world on a global scale. On a smaller scale, it aims to split churches, families, marriages, and even schools. In individuals, it produces divided hearts and double mindedness, making them unstable in many ways.*

"Its goal is to weaken humanity and make people easier to overtake. This spirit is responsible for political division, doctrinal disputes, the Civil War, vaccine conflicts, and movements like BLM. Its only plan is to destroy humanity through self-destruction. It is a confederacy of dishonor, rebellion, disunity, and disharmony."

Chapter 5
Portals and Pillars

In our world, the supernatural realm plays a vital role in shaping society and influencing the atmospheres of certain places. Some locations feel joyous, happy, and full of love, while others feel heavy, eerie, or dark. As I engaged Heaven one day for revelation about why this is, I became aware that many portals are scattered across the Earth. Heaven revealed that there are godly portals—heavenly access points from which the glory of the Lord shapes culture. Some of these have been overtaken and transformed into ungodly portals through theft, profane practices, or corruption by the spread of darkness upon the Earth. As a result, these distort the very essence of the land.

Seeking to understand more, I inquired of the Lord about their purposes and Heaven's strategies for redeeming them for the Kingdom.

I was shown Romans 8:19–21:

For the earnest expectation of the creation eagerly waits for the revealing of the sons of God. For the creation was subjected to futility, not willingly, but because of Him who subjected it in hope; because the creation itself also will be delivered from the bondage of corruption into the glorious liberty of the children of God.

As I heard this, I inquired about Tibet—known not only for its breathtaking landscapes but also for the occultism embraced there through yoga and New Age practices. Heaven said, "There is both a portal and a pillar of the Earth there."

I was shown that pillars are constructs in our plane of existence that act as amplifiers or power centers by which the Earth vibrates at the frequency of the dimension we inhabit. This is the groaning represented in Romans 8:22:

For we know that the whole creation groans and labors with birth pangs together until now.

These pillars are not merely natural formations; they are foundations woven into creation itself. They connect to the celestial and heavenly realms and serve as stabilizing power centers for both mankind and the spiritual environments of the regions they occupy.

However, their sanctity can be threatened. If they become surrounded by darkness, their energy may turn negative. Instead of radiating life and light, a corrupted pillar may emit frequencies of gloom and despair. This disturbs the delicate balance of the environment, affecting not only nature but also the hearts and minds of the people nearby.

Heaven said, *"When a pillar is taken over by surrounding darkness, its frequencies can be corrupted, and it can give off resonant frequencies of darkness."*

Restoring this imbalance can be achieved through prayer for the nations and by asking the Father to send angels to demolish strongholds erected in the high places that corrupt these portals and pillars.

These actions are essential for restoring purity to the pillars and renewing the Kingdom influence intended to surround them. By understanding the significance of these portals and pillars around the world, we step into a journey of transformation, becoming the sons of God who are destined to help deliver creation from bondage.

Portal of Power

As I sought Heaven for wisdom about portals, I was brought before a gate called *the Portal of Power.* When I stepped into its glorious golden and white light, I saw flashes like memories—or video clips—of great revivals and mighty men and women of God performing powerful works on Earth, moving in signs, wonders, and miracles.

While I stood marveling at these scenes, I felt as though I were moving on a conveyor belt. At the same time, my body tingled with what felt like static electricity.

I arrived at a place where I seemed to be watching a video of something yet to come. I saw myself, my family, and others standing in a small village that resembled Guatemala. We were praying for people. The villagers were amazed—both by hearing the true gospel of Jesus Christ and by witnessing God's miraculous power. A small blind boy was prayed for, and creative miracles unfolded: he grew new eyeballs and began to see. The villagers stood in awe and wonder, and my team wept, overwhelmed by God's goodness, giving Him praise for the works He had done.

As I continued in this realm, my personal angel, Philip, accompanied me. He explained that this was more than a viewing portal—it was a charging station, an impact portal for the anointing. I was reminded of Jesus' promise to His disciples that they would walk in greater power through the Holy Spirit.

> *Most assuredly, I say to you, he who believes in Me, the works that I do he will do also; and greater works than these he will do, because I go to My Father.* (John 14:12)

This place symbolized the fulfillment of that promise—preserving records of the past while prophesying their fulfillment in the future. It was a realm where the winds of revival swept over visitors, energizing their spirits and equipping them for Heaven's calling: to bring revival and testify to Christ's miracle-working power.

Prophesying Portals

During another conversation with Heaven, the Holy Spirit gave this instruction: *"What you speak out opens a portal."*

I pictured myself speaking a prophetic word. In the supernatural realm, a ring of light appeared—an entryway into the spoken word. The Holy Spirit said, *"Now step through it by faith."*

When I walked through the shimmering portal, I found myself in a lovely garden at the edge of a green forest. Brilliant flowers of every shade swayed in the breeze. Warm wind brushed my skin, carrying the sweet fragrance of blossoms. Golden sunlight filtered through the leaves above, casting playful shadows. It felt like stepping into a piece of paradise—nature's beauty forming a sanctuary of peace, wonder, and promise.

Bilocation & Pocket Realms

As I continued to journey in the seer dimension, I found myself standing under a shower of living waters from Heaven. I realized this shower was actually a fountain in a heavenly business complex. An atrium and elevators stood before me, much like those in an office building.

The Holy Spirit instructed me, *"Go to the seventh floor."*

When I reached the elevator, I noticed its glass enclosure, allowing me to see the entire complex as I ascended. On the seventh floor was a large, empty office space with a structure in the center resembling a transport portal.

Philip explained that this portal could transport me anywhere in the heavenly realm. From the windows, I saw the Healing Gardens, the Court Complex, the Father's House, and other realms—each visible from different vantage points.

After speaking with him, I stepped onto the portal and was instantly transported to an old cabin in the woods. Inside was what I call a "glory shower." When you stand beneath it, the radiance of the Father's glory pours over you, refreshing your spirit.

In that moment I received revelation about bilocation. In the spirit, you can occupy two places at once. My spirit remained on the seventh floor speaking with Philip while I simultaneously walked through the wilderness and stood in the cabin under the glory shower. It felt like a split screen, yet both experiences were fully real.

Then my spirit returned to one location, revealing how spiritual positioning and travel function.

I was then taught about pocket realms and how they can open in and out of time and space as both offensive and defensive strategies against the adversary.

The Five Pillars of Anointing

One April morning, tired and weak after a weekend of witnessing God's miraculous works, my spirit was alive but my body exhausted. In prayer I fought off a strange fever. All I wanted was to be in the Lord's presence. I made my way to the couch, turned on worship music, and began seeking Heaven.

As I looked into the realms, I saw five towers of light before me. Heaven revealed they were *the Five Pillars of Anointing*. Each served as an amplifier to expand Heaven's flow throughout creation: **intimacy, intercession, revival, revelation, and faith.**

Through these pillars, the frequencies of Heaven were amplified and sent into creation, like white light refracting through a prism. I heard Heaven say, "The anointing brings transformation, breaks chains, removes demons, heals, reveals, spreads the Father's love, and draws hearts to repentance."

Many are anointed and called by God, but few truly flow from the anointing and labor in the glory realms.

I recognized my earlier self in this. Fear lived in me then. I would grow tired and worn after ministering. Those around me felt the same—exhausted after deliverance sessions. This was not the glory; it was ministry from human effort.

Heaven then showed how things had shifted because of an insatiable hunger for fellowship with God and the desire to enter Heaven's realms. When we enter the secret place *and minister from unlimited anointing*, we do not grow weary or overthink. We operate from the limitless resources of the Father.

Heaven said, "Let the glory be the place where you stand as a representative of the Kingdom. Sit at the right hand of the Father as you are given, rule, and reign. Bring Heaven to Earth, and what will manifest will be awe-inspiring."

The anointing comes by invitation, and from invitation comes activation. Heaven said, "Cry out to be filled, beloved, and wait for the Lord to pour out the beauty of His presence in your life."

It is from this place that we see the greatness of the abundant life of Christ.

The Forest of Truth

In another vision, I found myself in a realm called *the Forest of Truth*. Lush greenery and tall trees surrounded me. I was told this forest is an access point in the spirit where many gates and portals can be entered through the Father's truth.

I entered one that led to *the place of rest*. It resembled a private Caribbean island—palm trees, serene surroundings, turquoise water, and a lounge chair in the sand. Rest could be accessed here much like resting on a beach.

Next, I was taken to *the place of access*—a divine superhighway of light where beams poured down from above. This realm provided access to wisdom and knowledge that flowed from the Father to the saints.

Chapter 6
The Father's Nature

As we outgrow the lies that religion would have us believe about the Father and learn His true nature, we often discover that God is not a God of punishment but One of everlasting grace, mercy, and love. During a season when I was being decontaminated from religious upbringing, I encountered the Father's kindness in a new way and began to understand His true compassionate nature.

One morning, I was taken into a vision where I was reminded of a key the Father had given me during a past encounter. Suddenly, the matching keyhole appeared out of nowhere. I inserted the key and turned it, but it vanished instantly. Then a doorway appeared, leading to a place of peace—a refuge the Father described as being like the Secret Place, a sanctuary where I could escape from all the fears of the world and simply experience His rest.

This place looked like a beach with white sand, clear blue water, waves crashing upon the shore, and the scent of ocean mist. The Father reminded me of *Jeremiah 29:11* and showed me the first time He placed that Scripture before my eyes. I was in a state of brokenness. My wife was having my daughter, and we were struggling in our relationship; it was a terribly painful time in my life. The Scripture said,

> *I know the plans that I have for you; plans of prosperity and peace, not of disaster.*

When the Father first gave me this Scripture, I could not have imagined how many times His goodness would fulfill it in the years to come. He restored my wife and family to me. And as if that were not enough, He fulfilled the dreams of my youth—marriage, a son, a daughter, and a joyful family of my own. Beyond that, He blessed me with five children.

The Father showed me that His promises to fill you are true—whether once or ten times, whether you have followed Him for thirty years or thirty seconds. He is faithful; He loves us, and nothing can separate us from that love. His faithfulness endures forever.

Revelation of Revival

One morning while I was worshiping in church, I felt surrounded by the presence of Heaven. As I looked in the spirit, I saw prophets gathered within the Cloud of Witnesses—Elijah, Elisha, Ezekiel, and Isaiah. Each one shared profound wisdom from Heaven. In that moment, I felt an overwhelming sense of love as I looked toward Jesus and the Father. They encouraged me to rise above the distractions of this world. Then I saw myself through Their eyes, wearing a crown in Their glorious Kingdom.

I sensed the weight of the Lord's Spirit descending into our natural realm. Waves of divine glory flowed out from our church, spilling over Long Island and radiating outward across the Earth. Suddenly, the ground beneath me shook violently. Long Island quivered as I heard a word accompanied by the number *6.0*—the approaching wave of a catastrophic tsunami.

The Earth cracked open, and the sky shifted chaotically. Looking downward, I saw lava and fire, along with dark shadows of desperate souls plunging into the abyss—many were lost.

Yet amid the chaos, I lifted my eyes to the split sky, where an astonishingly bright light poured forth. Before me stood the Father upon His majestic throne. A multitude gathered before Him; many souls from Earth were being drawn into this magnificent light. I saw myself standing before the throne upon a sea of glass, shimmering like crystal.

As waves of divine glory crashed upon the church, I felt the intensity rise through five powerful waves, then five more—overwhelming me with the profound presence of God. This was not just a moment; it was an encounter that would forever change my life and shape my faith.

Beloved

On another occasion, I had a profound encounter with the Lord while driving to work. He revealed to me the depth of His love—how cherished I am as His beloved, along with all His children.

In that moment, I felt enveloped in His embrace, surrounded by galaxies, cradled as tenderly as a newborn. He reminded me of the first time I held my daughter and urged me to magnify that experience an uncountable number of times beyond human understanding—*that* is how favored I am in His sight.

I was undone by His love, weeping uncontrollably in gratitude for His goodness.

Taking my hand, Jesus led me through Heaven's hospital, where He performed surgery on my heart, removing shards of glass, arrows, pins, and every hidden wound. I felt as if I were on an operating table, watching angels, Jesus, and the Father gather around me. Then I saw myself clothed in radiant white, wearing gleaming golden armor.

In another vision, He showed me a mantle of fire flowing behind me like a cloak, igniting the ground as I walked. He explained that this symbolized a season of prophetic growth—much like the tumultuous teenage years—and that this was the stage I was walking through with Him.

Every time His voice echoed the word *"Beloved,"* I wept even more at His goodness. By the time I arrived at work, I was utterly undone—overflowing with joy, stumbling under the weight of the Holy Spirit, dropping my keys and coat, uncaring and overwhelmed by the Father's love.

Hope for the Holidays

During a major turning point in my life, I began asking the Lord what He wanted me to learn in that season. In His grace, He brought me back to memories from years before I had accepted the gift of salvation. It was a dark time when the holiday season—a time meant for joy—felt instead like a cloak of sorrow.

In a vision, I saw my life in chaos; it felt as though every precious thing had been stripped away. I had wandered into deep darkness, caught in destructive habits and weighed with sin. I lost my home, my family, and even my hope. My existence felt hollow.

In the midst of that darkness, a thought pierced through—my Father's gentle voice urging me toward holiness. He believed that if I followed that sacred path, I could become a light for others who were lost in their battles.

My heart ached for those who carried the weight of past hurts during a season meant for celebration. In that quiet moment, the Holy Spirit whispered to my heart, reminding me of the power of Jesus—the Light of the World—who dispels all darkness.

But I also realized something important: even those who bear God's name can experience sorrow so heavy that it dims the light within.

A stirring awakened in my spirit—a calling to break chains of trauma that had imprisoned my family and many others. I longed to bring healing to the sons and daughters of God who felt trapped in sadness. As the Festival of Lights approached, I was reminded of my mission: to shine as a beacon of hope for those in darkness.

I wanted my life to be like an arrow pointing others back to their heavenly home—my ministry and words igniting hope, reminding them of the light shining through every hardship. I committed to remain open to the gentle guidance of the Holy Spirit, believing everything would unfold as He intended.

That journey transformed how I viewed the holidays and reshaped my purpose—to bring hope to the hopeless and lead them from darkness into the warmth of God's love.

Tenderness

One morning, as I sat with the Lord in the secret place, my spirit cried out, *"Father, I want to know You as the Tender Shepherd."*

I was taken into a vision where I saw Him walking in a meadow, shepherd's staff in hand, watching over a flock of lambs. Joy radiated from His face as He looked upon them. One little lamb stumbled and fell, unable to rise. He walked gently toward it. The lamb cried out. The Father picked it up, cradling it within His loving embrace as He continued walking with the flock.

As I watched, emotion overwhelmed me, and I wept. I felt His tenderness pouring into the deepest parts of my being. He said, *"This lamb is you."*

I watched as the Father rubbed its head and caressed its neck, comforting it with steady reassurance. The lamb stirred uncertainly, yet the Father never wavered. He whispered peace and encouraged it to rest in His arms. Then He began humming a melody.

The Holy Spirit said, *"This is the melody of the Father's Sweet Embrace."*

He rocked the lamb gently like a newborn. The lamb relaxed, closed its eyes, and rested peacefully in His arms.

Heaven said we are like this lamb—His sheep, His children—those who stumble and fall. Yet He always scoops us up with tenderness and comfort. His nature never changes.

Heaven said, "Our souls get stuck expecting punishment and condemnation. We wrestle to understand how loving He truly is—how forgiving. We read the Word and claim to understand grace, but do we really?

"Do we still carry unbelief that He is kind? Have past wounds from religion or relationships convinced us that love must sting? Do we secretly fear that the Father is waiting to punish us?

"Do you have the fear of the Lord—or a fear **of** the Lord?"

> *The fear of the Lord is the beginning of wisdom, And the knowledge of the Holy One is understanding.* (Proverbs 9:10)

True "fear of the Lord" is love-born reverence—like the Shulamite's devotion in Song of Solomon. It keeps us near Him, not running away.

If we fear intimacy with Him, we have embraced the lie of religion. That lie opens the door to the deceiver, for Satan is the one who harms. The Father desires to reward us with unfailing love.

Thoughts like *"God must be punishing me"* or constant fear of failure are symptoms of a distorted view of His character. Shame, guilt, and dread are not His tools; fear is not one of the Seven Spirits of God. The Father's nature is compassion, mercy, and unending love.

Scripture appeared:

A father is tender and kind to his children. In the same way, the Lord is tender and kind to those who have respect for Him. (Psalm 103:13, NIRV)

I was reminded of the parable of the prodigal son. The passage unfolded before me:

So the young son set off for home. From a long distance away, his father saw him coming, dressed as a beggar, and great compassion swelled up in his heart for his son who was returning home. The father raced out to meet him, swept him up in his arms, hugged him dearly, and kissed him over and over with tender love.

Then the son said, 'Father, I was wrong. I have sinned against you. I could never deserve to be called your son. Just let me be—'

The father interrupted and said, 'Son, you're home now!'

Turning to his servants, the father said, 'Quick, bring me the best robe, my very own robe, and I will place it on his shoulders. Bring the ring, the seal of sonship, and I will put it on his finger. And bring out the best shoes you can find for my son.

'Let's prepare a great feast and celebrate. For my beloved son was once dead, but now he's alive! Once he was lost, but now he is found!' And everyone celebrated with overflowing joy. (Luke 15:20–24, TPT)

Like the prodigal, we struggle to accept grace because we focus on our past—the very past washed away by Jesus' blood. We must choose to release ourselves so shame does not blind us to His tenderness.

When we submit to this truth, we find peace in His arms, even if we fell moments ago. His nature is to love beyond our limits, reassure us, and comfort us even when we sit in the mess. His grace is everlasting; His lovingkindness never ends.

If we surrender to His gentleness, kindness, and embrace, we will find rest for our weary souls.

Prayer: *Holy Spirit, tenderize our hearts so we may experience the tenderness of the Father.*

Theft of Time

After a long day, as I lay down trying to catch my breath, I heard the small, still voice of the Lord beckoning to me.

"Be still, My child be still, you were learning new and powerful strategies to fight back. The forces of darkness are working hard to steal time from the Saints."

I had just spent part of the evening in prayer with another seer, entering into the Celestial Court of Heaven to reclaim what the enemy had stolen. The angels in this court warned us that the enemy's forces were trying to claim generational blessings and had stolen time and provision from our ancestors. As we entered prayer, we presented our case before the Ancient of Days and, upon receiving justice, asked for all that was lost or stolen to be returned.

Although victorious in the courts, my soul was troubled by the everyday worries of life. By faith, I instructed my spirit to draw from the rivers of living water in the gardens of Heaven to bring peace to my tired soul, and I could feel relief coming. I was taken back in time, feeling as if things were being rewound to specific moments when healing and other blessings were meant to be released to me but had not yet been.

Unraveling of Time

The next evening, while I was in deep intercession and prayer for a friend, Heaven revealed to me a long-standing strategy of hell called the *Unraveling of Time and Timelines*.

When I asked what this meant, Heaven replied, "The enemy attempts to steal the sequencing of time based on what the Father has allotted for His children to receive, steward, or walk in at a specific moment.

"This strategy is especially effective on the wayward sons—those marching to the beat of their own drum. They are unaware of the work of the Father's hands and do not seek His face for His purposes in their lives. Likewise, many who are called sons of God do not pursue the Father intimately enough to understand the timing of the blessings they are meant to inherit."

Have you ever received a prophetic word and felt as if it never came to pass? Many experience this—missing the fulfillment because they did not engage with the word at the appointed time or did not labor in prayer to bring it into the natural realm. God is not a man that He should lie, yet the timing of the release or the harvesting of a seed can be delayed.

These delays place a person on a path where time stretches abnormally. In that stretch, the enemy sneaks in, deceives the believer, and plants seeds of doubt. Much like the serpent in the Garden of Eden, the deceiver disrupts divine timing.

Suddenly, the Scripture unfolded before me:

> *Now the serpent was more cunning than any beast of the field which the Lord God had made. And he said to the woman, 'Has God indeed said, "You shall not eat of every tree of the garden?"' And the woman said to the serpent, 'We may eat the fruit of the trees of the garden; but of the fruit of the tree which is in the midst of the garden, God has said, "You shall not eat it, nor shall you touch it, lest you die."' Then the serpent said to the woman, 'You will not surely die. For God knows that in the day you eat of it your eyes will be opened, and you will be like God, knowing good and evil.'* (Genesis 3:1–5)

As seen here, the serpent convinced Eve she would not die. Though she did not die immediately, a fracture occurred in the original design that the first Adam embodied. This rupture unraveled the integrity of mankind's timeline, leading to their expulsion from Eden, a fall from grace, and the onset of mortality across the human race.

I was puzzled, and a couple of my angels laughed gently as I tried to understand. I asked, "But doesn't God know all things from the beginning?"

The Holy Spirit replied, *"Yes. Heaven is always ten steps ahead of hell. But the power of agreement allows people to choose a lesser inheritance, which can unravel the structure of time they were meant to operate in."*

As I listened, I saw something like a ball of thread unspooling.

Heaven said, "These are the strands of time. They are part of the makeup of the timeline. When they become tangled or unraveled, chaos can begin to operate in a person's life.

"By partnering with your angels and praying from the Courts of Heaven, you can address this strategy quickly and receive Heaven's help in restoring order. Simply enter the Court of Times and Seasons, repent for where time was unraveled through agreements with the enemy's lies, and ask for time to be restored to the Father's original design.

"God is a Lover of second chances. Be mindful that time is both a tool and a precious resource. Steward your time wisely and guard your heart against the lies of the wicked one."

Soar

On the morning of December 24, 2023, I was in prayer after finishing a devotional on *1 Timothy 2:5* and intercessory prayer. The devotional included an excerpt from *Dark Night of the Soul* by St. John of the Cross, the sixteenth-century Spanish mystic. As I meditated on these things, I looked in the Spirit and saw a phoenix rising from the ashes of religion.

The Holy Spirit explained that this phoenix was a metaphor for how the Lord sees me—as someone of great strength and power, refined by His fire and enriched by His might. Then He said, *"The height at which this phoenix flies is the height at which you soar in the Spirit."*

Suddenly His voice poured over me again, *"Fly up, son of God, into the highest Heavens—into the highest heights—beyond accusation and the arrow of delay, beyond judgment and criticism, beyond the razor-sharp teeth of religion, and above the hurts of the soul-ruled realm called Earth.*

"Your spirit is far more mature than your earthly years, and your mind has adapted to a mystic mindset. You walk as a son and friend of God the Father. Your path will not be understood by others, nor will they share in the joy of the knowledge and revelation I release through you, but My Word will always be the lamp to your feet, lighting this path.

"Seek first the Kingdom, and you will not be misled by feelings caused by the immaturity and offenses of others you meet. My burden is easy, My yoke is light, and I say to you: take hold of My promises and seize the day with the sword of the Spirit in your hand. Strike down oppressors and opposition with a kind word and loving correction.

"Come dwell in My house, and all shall be well. I am so pleased with your progress and how you walk. Do not be disappointed or ashamed, for your calling is different, and others may not understand or may reject it. But in My Kingdom, beloved son, you are fully accepted."

As these words washed over me, Scripture unfolded before my eyes:

> *But those who wait on the Lord shall renew their strength; they shall mount up with wings like eagles, they shall run and not be weary, they shall walk and not faint.* (Isaiah 40:31)

This encounter marked a defining moment in my spiritual journey—an invitation to rise above earthly limitations and soar in the Spirit according to the height of His calling.

Chapter 7
Understanding Frequencies

Frequencies are woven into everything God created. They are the resonance of His voice—the echo of the Word that spoke all things into existence. Every created thing carries a sound, a vibration, and a frequency, just as a living body carries breath, pulse, and flowing blood.

Like any created force, frequencies can be used for good or harm—to build up or tear down, to attract or repel. As I pondered this, I suddenly found myself in a classroom. A man dressed in radiant white, named Luther, appeared. He held a stick of chalk and, without speaking, lifted his hand, curled his fingers slightly, and scraped his nails down the chalkboard.

The sound made me instinctively recoil, yet my spirit remained at peace. Luther explained, "This is a picture of a distorted and unpleasant frequency."

Frequencies can disrupt or interfere with the God-ordained function and order of a person, place, or thing. For example, arrhythmias are disturbances in the heart rate. Another common condition caused by changes in frequencies is arterial fibrillation. These alter the patterns and sounds of the heart's rhythm and can lead to problems within the body. When frequencies shift in the human body, they can throw things off course or bring them back into Heaven's divine design.

I asked, "How can I use frequencies to help heal and minister?"

Luther replied, "You can call tuning angels into situations where frequency adjustments are needed, and they can help reset and restore them. There is also a department in Heaven's healing hospital where frequencies can be fine-tuned, and scans can identify ungodly frequencies and the issues they cause. Simply check a patient in, follow Heaven's guidance regarding the dysfunction, and request that the frequencies be restored to emulate the song of the Lord."

Walk with wisdom and understanding as you continue to explore these topics. The world has greatly corrupted their meanings for the body, but in this hour, this day, and this age, it is the Father's intention that His sons reclaim what the enemy has stolen and walk rightly in the abundant riches of Heaven.

Working with Frequencies from the Quantum Essence Realm

As I engaged with Heaven one Saturday morning after a week-long battle with my health, I found it hard to press into the presence of God. My soul was weary, my thoughts racing, my body was worn out, and I was feeling flustered. I wondered why I was experiencing such hardship. I could feel my heart so burdened inside my chest, and I asked the Father what was going on with me. I started questioning, wondering what the issue was. Did I have side effects from medications? Sleeplessness? Had I been striving too much?

Suddenly, the Father's voice broke through my conscious though process. He said, *"My son, tune to the flow of Heaven."*

I took a breath and aligned my realms, placing my spirit first. Immediately, I saw waterfalls in Heaven. I pressed in for more and heard children laughing. A small boy was drying a puppy that had just had a bath, flinging bubbles everywhere. Then I heard birds singing and felt the warmth of summer sunshine.

The Father said, *"These are a few of my favorite things."*

As I continued to lean in, He lifted me onto His lap. I became like a small child as He placed His hands gently on my back, applying light pressure to calm me.

He said, *"My son, the devil himself will appear to you burdening you with business. Do not be burdened under Satan's yolk, rather, be wise to his strategies and overcome them with heavenly resources."*

As He said these things He clapped His hands twice and attendants entered the room.

We were in the Throne Room. Before us stood three men in white: Mitchell, Malcom & Michael. I recognized Mitchell and Malcolm from previous encounters. Michael introduced himself as a "professor of spiritual sciences."

They brought with them a smart board on wheels and a large ancient-looking book. Its leather cover was worn and dusted with age, and its gold-embossed title read: *The Power of Frequency.*

The Father said, *"I believe it's time we unravel this mystery for him."*

Those present chuckled softly as I stood there, still bewildered. Michael turned toward me and asked, *"What do you know about frequency?"*

I replied, "Well, I think I know quite a bit—but I have a feeling that what I know pales in comparison to what we're about to learn."

He smiled slightly. *"You are correct."*

Michael continued, *"Frequency is one of the most powerful things ever created."*

That statement stirred questions in me. I thought, *Frequency... part of creation itself?*

> *And then God announced, 'Let there be light,' and light burst forth!* (Genesis 1:3, TPT)

Michael continued, "Frequency was used by God to speak all things into existence. Every created thing carries a frequency—a sound wave. Sound waves create vibration.

"Just as the earth's atmosphere contains positive and negative ions that influence storms and lightning, there are positive and negative frequencies that can either empower or dampen the flow of the anointing—and life itself."

He looked at me more intently and continued, "Just as ions can affect the human body, frequencies can affect the human spirit. You've recently been taught about the quantum essence realm—the Father's essence. This realm carries a specific frequency that shifts the atmosphere and produces conditions where faith thrives and creative miracles occur."

I blinked a few times, trying to take it in. "Can you simplify that for me?"

Mitchell stepped forward. "Think about what happens when you mix baking soda and vinegar."

"You get a chemical reaction—it fizzes and bubbles," I answered.

"Exactly," he said. "Frequency works the same way. When you introduce frequency into a situation, it causes a reaction—positive or negative.

"When you have faith for something, and you pray and then see the answer manifest, you've mixed faith with hope... and added frequency through prayer. The result is manifestation. When the Father created all things, He spoke through frequency and through His essence—His glory—and creation was birthed."

"Now, consider a negative example. When someone lives in fear or worry, they release a negative frequency that weights them down. The enemy feeds off these frequencies—they smell like rot and sewage in the spirit realm. The moment someone comes into agreement with negativity, the enemy pushes further, feeding lies and torment, which can spiral into panic, chaos, and even destruction. These frequencies have fueled violence, war, and death across the earth."

Malcolm handed me a folder. When I opened it, a holographic document appeared in the room—a teaching by Dr. Ron Horner on positive and negative frequencies.

Heaven impressed me: *When we operate in Heaven's higher frequencies, environments shift. As we speak these frequencies, we prophesy life over our destiny.*

Michael stated, "When you release Heaven's frequencies, be intentional. What you speak manifests because you are a son of God. Try it."

I opened my mouth and declared, "I am blessed and highly favored.

"I am filled with the joy of the Lord—His joy is my strength."

As I spoke, I felt a shift. A buzzing sensation moved through me, lifting my heart. Joy erupted.

Heaven said, "What you feel is vibration. Frequencies produce vibration, and vibration shifts you—and the reality around you. Heaven's vibrational frequencies work with the quantum essence realm to bring transformation."

Mitchell asked, "How well are you understanding these things?"

I answered, "They are new—yet somehow familiar."

"Good," he said. "Let us continue."

The Antichrist Frequency

Mitchell began, "Be careful about which frequencies you allow into your eye and ear gates; frequencies open portals: foul language and hateful speech open portals of destruction and negative influence. Be diligent to control these realms and keep them closed. Use the aid of your angels with grey capture bags for extra security in removing negative frequencies.

"Negative frequencies added to other negative frequencies are like throwing water on a grease fire—junk will spray everywhere, and the flames will get out of control. We share this because it is one of hell's most effective strategies on earth today. In this age, frequencies of disrespect, rebellion, dishonor, hatred, disharmony, fear, death, and disunity are being intentionally fed to the masses, as Satan tries to enslave humanity because his time is running out. These are antichrist frequencies.

"The antichrist frequency is still common in today's society. It is very damaging to generational DNA, keeping many stuck in deep religious cycles that believe lies. It prevents God's children from reaping their true rewards and seeing their inheritance by reinforcing religious and poverty lies. This frequency causes jealousy and envy over others' blessings, mocks and rejects others' revelations and testimonies, and worse, promotes pride and arrogance in the face of mercy and love. The antichrist frequency attempts to shut down the anointing and flow within the body of Christ, rendering the bride powerless and unable to fulfill her calling in this hour. There is a need for the sons of God to rise up, restore the body, and equip the bride to regain her authority. This frequency must be extinguished immediately so that doubt, hopelessness, and faithlessness do not prevail, leading to the second death (spiritual death).

"As you learn to flow with the quantum essence realm, it is imperative to live out of this realm of the Glory. As you live from this place and carry it with you, speak out the frequencies of the Kingdom to those around you, bless others, do acts of loving kindness to them, live by the fruit of the Spirit, for these are the chain-breaking frequencies."

> *But the fruit produced by the Holy Spirit within you is divine love in all its expressions: overflowing joy, calming peace, enduring patience, active kindness, virtuous living, prevailing faith, gentle hearts, and spiritual strength. Never put the law above these qualities, for they are meant to be limitless.* (Galatians 5:22-23, TPT)

Michael said, "The goodness of God flows through frequency, and as you bring quantum shifts into lives through others by using the power of frequency to deliver all creation, His goodness will win souls and bring the lost back from the worship of Baal."

> *Or do you despise the riches of His goodness, forbearance, and longsuffering, not knowing that the goodness of God leads you to repentance?* (Romans 2:4)

The Father said, *"This is wisdom for the ages, my son. Be careful to guard your tongue and let the Holy Spirit be set as a seal upon your heart and your mouth. For as a son, what you speak you shall have the fruit of; what words you sow shall be the harvest that you reap. Keep your speech unblemished and undefiled by godless, unfruitful mysticism and prophecy—life over all things. Speak words of life and great value over your family, your business affairs, your faith, and your homes. Speak words of great value over your enemies and adversaries—not with scorn, but with mercy and compassion, for their needs are great. The hours are soon to come, when their reward shall be served to them."* As the Father spoke, I nodded.

Mitchell said, a final caution, added, "Those in leadership—prophets, heads of households, families, and homes—give ear. Let these words be stored in your heart: bless and do not curse; build up and do not tear down; sow seeds of mercy, not scorn. When you speak this way, the Father's voice can be heard through you. The adversary, the devil, has long used the antichrist frequency to turn the hearts of the masses against hearing the Father and knowing His goodness."

> *In fact, the mind-set focused on the flesh fights God's plan and refuses to submit to his direction, because it cannot!* (Romans 8:7, TPT)

Do not be the source of further burden to them, but deliver them in love. Prophecy over their lives as if it were your own child stuck in the world and headed toward spiritual death, that they too may be saved and attend the wedding feast of the Lamb by your sides.

The Process

I asked if there is a process we should learn to handle negative frequencies. Malcom said there isn't a formal process, like one used in court, but rather being assertive, confident in God, and standing fully in authority—knowing that as you speak, the frequencies of Heaven will overtake negative frequencies and shift atmospheres.

A few simple strategies, however, that may be helpful for personal advocacy, intercession, and working with others, are as follows:

- You can call upon the tuning fork angels to retune their bodily frequencies to those of Heaven in the Court of Angels.
- Heaven's Healing Hospital has a frequency healing center. You can enter this place and ask for the angels of purity to cleanse and purify your DNA and

generational lines from all negative and anti-Christ frequencies. Afterward, ask to be attuned or retuned to Heaven's frequencies.

- Last but not least, practice on your own: align your realms and quantum realms. Prophecy to open a portal and step into it. Instruct the glory to stand up and arise within you.

I paused, realigned my realms, instructed the glory to rise, and extended my hand forward. I opened my mouth and said, "In Jesus' name, portal of joy, open up." In the Spirit, I saw a blue-white ring of fire swirling around a portal, and the light in the center resembled liquid metal. By faith, I stepped into it. As I entered, I felt very light, and it seemed like all the weight and heaviness I had been carrying just melted off my shoulders. I saw blueish-white fire all around, but not the kind that burns. I placed a hand on my belly, then on my heart, and said, "Portal of peace, open up." I could feel the instant vibrational shifts as my frequencies moved out of the earthly frequencies of worry and anxiety, replaced with Heaven's joy and peace.

The Father said to practice these things in all your affairs. The world is sick with sin, and many are seeking these keys in the world through access points of new age teachings, candy-coated fortunes, and occult rituals. They will never bear the fruit they need but will harvest the sap from the tree of which they seek. I asked, "Papa, do you mean they are harvesting death by choice?"

He looked at me and wept uncontrollably, nodding. As He wept over His lost sheep, I began to weep, and all of Heaven with us. With one hand, he dried His eyes and said, *"My beloved child, that is why you are being entrusted with these things in this hour. It is time to reclaim Kingdom truth and deliver the lost from the lies of independence, self-reliance, and selfishness."*

> *Those who are motivated by the flesh only pursue what benefits themselves. But those who live by the impulses of the Holy Spirit are motivated to pursue spiritual realities. For the sense and reason of the flesh is death, but the mind-set controlled by the Spirit finds life and peace.* (Romans 8:5-6, TPT)

As the engagement ended, Mitchell handed me the leather-bound book, and by faith, I received it into my heart so I could walk in the fullness of the newfound knowledge and revelation.

Chapter 8
The Battle for Peace

As I sat with the Lord in the secret place one morning, my soul was wrestling to be still I felt hard pressed on every side; I felt like things around me weren't going the way I had hoped or thought they would—family-wise, business-wise, financially, and even in ministry. My heart was hurting and broken, my thoughts racing and hinging on a place of worry. As I spoke softly to the Lord, I heard the Father's small, still voice speak to me, and He asked me a question.

The Father said, *"Do you know why you feel so crushed?"*

I answered no. At this moment, my mind was trying to figure it out, and my first inclination was, had I sinned? Was this an attack?

The Father spoke, *"You are in a place of humbling. You are on the verge of a massive breakthrough, but first, you must be completely humble and able to walk in what is coming your way. I am tearing down the pedestals, so that you don't exalt yourself and that no man exalts your works above Me. I do not want you to walk in an inflated air of self-importance; I want you to grow in God-reliance, knowing fully that all you have now was born out of nothing, and all you are coming into was born out of sonship. Trust in me, the Great I AM."*

He asked, *"How do you feel in this moment?"*

I said, "Like I can do nothing apart from You."

The Father answered, *"This is the posture of the sons; it is a humility you are to keep and teach. Many have fallen into the traps of lust of the eyes, lust of the flesh and the pride of life, but you, My son, shall not fall headlong into poverty and disgrace; you shall build My Kingdom and teach your descendants of my ways."*

I heard my personal angel, Phillip, say, "In all your ways acknowledge Him and He shall make all of your paths peace."

Frequency Disruptions

As I continued seeking guidance from Heaven, I received these instructions from the Holy Spirit, *"Don't be disturbed by the frequency disruptions you are experiencing. The days you are walking through are times known for heightened activity. They are high, unholy days for the kingdom of darkness. The evil of this age may overwhelm some, but for my sons, it is an age of redemption for all things. The presence of my sons on earth disrupts the plans of the enemy. The spoken Word and the walk of the righteous overthrow the schemes of hell. All that my children interact with see the glory of my image through the sons. Do not grow weary in your walk. The efforts of the wicked to subdue the righteous are futile. Their plans are pointless and will not divert you from my paths. Consider Elijah and the prophets of Baal. It is your duty to walk confidently in the hope I have given you, preach the gospel, bring hope to others, pray constantly without ceasing, and engage Heaven daily. This is the walk of a son; this is your inheritance and your path to victory. In everything, give glory to the Father. Seek the Kingdom of God early and often. Press into deeper revelation when you feel confined by natural circumstances. Your breakthrough is just around the corner.*

"My son you are indeed going through a crushing, a pressing and an expansion, your tent pegs have been lengthened, your territories are expanding and your finances exploding, the resources I have dealt you are increasing greatly. It is time to prune away the ugliness of past hurt, the defiling words and thoughts of your heart, and wash you clean in the Father's great love. Yield to the pain, let it strengthen your character, let it envelop you with fiery hot prayer... the holds of darkness are being broken off your life, your children, and the fire of God will devour every evil.

"My son you are arising into a greater authority in this season, know it or not, you are one who laughs in the face of

the devil, you are at war for My Kingdom, to win the souls of those who oppose you, to bring those called by My name to know that I am love... let the fire on your altar grow hotter than ever before. You, My child, are a man of magnificence. Rise up and stand in the greatness in which I am cultivating you to embody. Behold, the beauty of My Glory. Shine like the star that you are, beloved."

Protracted Peace

As I sought the Lord the next day my soul was in a state of distress. I had lost sight of the Lord's promises and was in a place of worry and self-will. As I heard the Holy Spirit beckon me to step into the heavenly realms, I started to see a destiny scroll laid out before me. It appeared as a view of a city from overhead. The Father said that the path I was intending with my will to walk on today was not His best and urged me to rethink my steps I was planning to take in regard to work, life and where I thought the best module for provision could be found. As I stared intently at this scroll looking at the buildings, the streets and even cars that were driving down these streets, it looked as if I was staring at a community of brown stone buildings like one would see in Brooklyn or the Bronx, circa 1940.

Suddenly I noticed what looked like a protractor measuring out specific lines, angles, and placements upon this scroll.

The Father called me, *"Jeremiah Joseph, you are both a weeping prophet like Jeremiah and one who will keep my storehouses and build like Joseph."*

He reminded me of a vision and word given to me in January 2023 about 7 storehouses I had in the spirit, and I saw them materialize on this scroll.

I heard the Father say, *"Heaven has many avenues to reach the intended place of expectation I have set before you."*

As the Father was speaking, I saw the street I was on was riddled with obstacles but at the end, was a path of "protracted peace." This peace was measured, marked out with precision by the Father Himself, inviting me to walk it with confidence.

What appeared as a gleaming golden stone, radiantly lit with creative light was ahead, and as I drew near it, I could feel it's warmth and the Father's joy. By faith I received this joy and the gift of the protracted peace of God into my realms. I could feel the peace of God and the Glory of the Lord rest upon me like a thin sheet falling on top of my back, head, and neck. As I gazed onward into Heaven, I saw a single reed, bending to the wind and then resetting itself, reaching upward toward the higher Heavens as if to call out and say, "I trust you, Lord."

Trust in the Lord completely, and do not rely on your own opinions. With all your heart rely on him to guide you, and he will lead you in every decision you make. Become intimate with him in whatever you do, and he will lead you wherever you go. (Proverbs 3:5-6, TPT)

Path to Peace

As the engagement continued, I heard the Lord say, *"You are in a period of refinement and purification. The feelings you experience are spiritual growing pains—caused when your soul tries to bottle up the emotions that seek to overwhelm and delay you from stepping forward into destiny. The way around this is continual spirit-forward living. Daily choose to die to self and yield to the flow of the Holy Spirit. Commission your angels to take captive every high-minded thought that exalts itself above the knowledge of God."*

I saw myself walking on a narrow, icy footpath suspended over a valley. There were no handrails, and I was gingerly making my way across the frozen path. I could see in my own posture the nervousness and anxiety rising in my body and soul. Suddenly, I saw Jesus walking toward me from the other side of the path. As He stepped forward, the ice melted beneath His feet. He extended His hand and pulled me into safety. He said sweetly, *"Allow My peace to remain."*

Abiding in the Peace of the Lord

On another occasion, as I stepped into Heaven, I saw beautiful white marble archways and columns; they were white marble stairways and beautiful sparkling crystal blue rivers of water, rivers of living water. I was told that this is a place of the habitation of the peace of the Lord. These living waters flow from the Throne of grace and mercy into the lives of all those that are the Father's. As I looked down, I saw an opening where all the rivers of water flow down like a waterfall into a chasm. I watched as they were poured out onto the saints on the Earth. As I observed this, I noticed that the living waters were electrified and full of the Father's fiery love.

In the spirit, Jesus took me by the hand and put me in these waters. In the natural, I could feel the flow of the glory all over my physical body.

The Lord spoke, *"My child, these waters cleanse and refresh the human spirit. They draw you back to your first love and the foundational understanding of the Father's pleasure—to be with His children, to be recognized by His children, to be loved and adored by His children, and to love and adore them in return. These waters also carry dreams, words of knowledge, prophecies, destinies, and everything the Father desires to release—what Heaven longs to trade into the lives of the Saints who receive them. They are poured out as freely as cisterns pour out water and are continually replenished with fresh water. These waters refresh the Saints and fill them up whenever they pray for the living waters to flow."*

As I looked upward, I saw many white clouds and mini arches of beautiful rainbows shimmering with radiant and brilliant colors in the skies above. Flocks of beautiful white birds and other heavenly creatures moved gracefully through the air, their sounds rising in praise to the Lord. The peace and joy in this place washed over me—overwhelming, restoring, and refreshing. Knowing we can come here in the spirit and receive this depth of rest left me completely undone.

Chapter 9
The Cost

One autumn morning, as I sat in the presence of God—soaking, weeping and praying—I heard Heaven speak, *"This walk is one you must take alone. The places I am bringing you to are higher than those around you are called to dwell. The river of revelation is flowing; the portals are open. This is a season of dreams, visions, new writings, and fresh encounters. Here, your decision to follow Me will be tested. Some days will be hard, others deeply fulfilling. You have prayed, 'Increase the anointing no matter the cost,' and I tell you today: your prayer has been answered. Do not grow faint of heart. I am with you in fire and in flood."*

As those words echoed through me, my focus was suddenly broken by the sound of heavy rain drumming on the roof. In that moment, I was taken into a vision of Noah's ark. I saw storm clouds churning above and floodwaters rising below, tossing the massive vessel in every direction. Waves hammered its starboard side, yet the ark never capsized. It remained upright through every surge.

Heaven said, *"My child, you are a ship—My vessel, a container of My glory, the Holy Spirit. Walk upright through every storm, every trial, every adversity. The days of this age grow increasingly dark, yet as the darkness presses in, My light shines all the brighter. Be the reason others do not lose hope. Open your mouth and release the fire. Strike down wickedness with nothing but a tongue and a prayer. Bless those who bless you. For those who curse you, pray for their salvation. Be swift to judge the thrones of wickedness in the heavenly places from My courts and bring freedom to My Bride.*

"The days are coming quickly when every knee will bow, and every tongue will confess the lordship of Jesus Christ. Yield to the burning of purification, for new oil is being produced. Let not your heart grow cold in love, though former hindrances have scorched it. Let neither hopelessness nor offense weaken your desire to seek Me wholeheartedly. Allow My hand to heal the broken places as I mold you into the man I chose you to be.

"The process is but the blink of an eye in eternity, though it shall span decades on earth. Press forward on this path of righteousness, for the ground you are taking is not only for you but for the fruit of your loins and for generations yet to come. The price you have paid will pave a clear way for them to possess the greater things of the Kingdom. What you have labored for will come easily to them—and even more easily to those who follow—for you, My son, have torn down the

walls that hindered relationship and worship and have plunged deeply into the depths of My love."

As I looked into the spirit, I saw many saints gathered around. Jesus was in the center, a hand on each shoulder. His eyes locked with mine. Around Him stood Moses, Abraham, Elijah, Melchizedek, multitudes of men clothed in white, and angels at His side. I fell to my knees before Him, and He spoke, *"Let the treasures of Heaven be poured richly upon you, and may all that I have spoken be established quickly in your days!"*

The Process of Pruning

As I lay prostrate another morning, seeking the Father's face, I felt broken, slimed and entangled in battles with the spirits of religion, offense, distraction, and compromise. I prayed a Psalm 51 prayer, inviting the Lord to correct the flawed places within me. Then I saw a vision: a rose, beautiful on the outside, yet from its center, smoke and magma burst upward like a volcano. The Holy Spirit said the eruption represented the anger beneath my surface, hidden beneath the beauty of the flower. I watched ash rise into a cloud as molten drops fell like burning rain. The Holy Spirit showed me this was a picture of what anger does to those around me when I allow it a place. "It hurts. It burns," I said aloud.

As I continued seeking the Father for healing and restoration of my heart, my spirit, and my walk with Him, I saw seven points in time—seasons of pruning I had walked through, each one cultivating deeper intimacy and greater awareness of God's depths and the presence of Heaven. These seven points appeared as ears of corn whose outer casings were being torn away, taking with them the dirt and dross. The ears were stripped from their stalks and their protective husks removed. What remained were pure white kernels on the cob, laid bare and ready for preparation.

"My son, this corn is a picture of your process—the continual stripping away of what is flesh, what is filth, and what does not belong. As you are laid bare, what remains is what I can work with: a pure vessel, a new wineskin, ready to be filled with the oil of purity and the new wine for which I have provided a perfect offering through the blood of Jesus. Lean into the fire. Lean into the pain. Lean into the pruning. This is a diamond day for you. No longer will you carry blemish or stain, darkened like coal. I am mining what is within you, cultivating a gifting and an intimacy that surpasses your current stature. Growth is painful, but it is worthwhile.

"As you move forward to lead My children out of darkness, I must first remove the darkness from your doorstep and expose every compromised place so that you may stand above reproach and worthy of the calling placed on you for this very hour. Walk tall, speak truth, and know

that I am deeply proud of you and profoundly in love with you, My beloved boy. Fear no evil, for I am with you. I have not abandoned you. Even in My silence, I am working in you and for you, to bring forth everything I have promised."

As the encounter faded, I heard Jesus whisper, *"The crushing of this season and the pressing you feel is for the purification of your heart. It will usher you into what comes next. The blessings ahead and the elevation the Father is bringing require a deeper level of submission and obedience to His direction. Yield to the Holy Spirit. Repent quickly when you fall into error. Return to the potter's wheel so that you may be reshaped and reformed into the manifest image of His glory.*

"Return to the altar of the Lord. Don't be counted among the Tares. The days are moving swiftly. The prodigals are coming home. Do not take this lightly. Not everyone who believes they are saved truly is. Be diligent in examining the posture of your heart. Repent, return, reconsecrate, and revive the practices that once kept your lamp filled with oil and your heart burning for the Kingdom. Beloved, guard your love for the light—let not the weeds of deception choke it out."

New Doors for a New Year

At the turn of the Hebrew year 5784 (Friday, September 15, 2023), I sat alone, seeking the Father's instruction. "What do You desire of me?"

He answered, *"All I require of you is your obedience, and I know I have it."*

As I listened, I saw the structures of my life—business, ministry, family—forming mountains all around me. Suddenly, a door of light opened at the center, and I walked through it into the mountains, to the Throne of the Lamb.

In the midst of the Throne Room was a whirlwind filled with doors opening. As it started to dissipate the doors were flung outwardly and arranged on a path before me. Jesus said this is significant for the year ahead. The doors were innumerable: some overflowing with harvest, some carrying music, others releasing financial provision.

Angels attended the doors, and members of my cloud of witnesses stood along the path holding gifts for appointed seasons—mantles, scrolls, revelations.

As I looked out over the sea of doors, I saw a company of angels before me. Two blew shofars, releasing frequencies of breakthrough and deliverance. The frequencies themselves were transformative. Two others lifted a rod between them, and I realized it was a large scroll—a scroll of destiny for this year and this season. As I stepped onto it, I found myself standing at a midpoint and wondered why the new year is celebrated in the seventh Hebrew month. Immediately, I understood the timelessness of eternity and the precision of prophecy: when the Lord speaks to us in time, His word aligns with an earthly sequence, though in eternity all things are already complete. From the Father's vantage, we're even now in unified worship before the King of Kings and Lord of Lords.

Later that day, I went to the store to buy challah and grape juice for our Rosh Hashanah dinner. I passed an end cap decorated with pumpkins and bundles of wheat. The Holy Spirit instructed me to purchase the wheat. As I got into my car, the Lord said, *"This wheat is a sign: you will experience great harvest in a short time."* I remembered Joseph's dream and also the word the Lord had spoken to me this past year—that I am a Joseph, being brought from the pit into the palace.

Green Pastures

The next morning, as I engaged Heaven, my first inclination was to check with my angels. I paused, waiting to observe what was unfolding. At first, I saw white streamers and ribbons drifting in the air, then ticker tape fluttering like confetti. As my vision sharpened, I realized I was at a parade.

I asked the Holy Spirit its meaning. He said, *"This is a celebration of the Father—Jehovah, the Most High God."* As He spoke, it resonated deeply within me. Simultaneously, I heard an African worship song in my spirit: "You are the Most High."

This parade celebrated every tribe and nation represented in Heaven, all worshipping the Father in unity. There was dancing, singing, and joy filled the atmosphere. No one stood still; everyone was engaged in this lavish outpouring of love and adoration for the Father.

Suddenly, I found myself on a parade float beside the Father and Jesus. The Father placed His hand on my shoulder and said, *"My son, your heart has grown dim under the pressure and burdens of life. Come release them and be refreshed today."*

As He spoke, I felt a sense of ease in my body; this was not just a verbal invitation but an impartation and activation of His rest and renewal.

He pulled my head to His chest and held me close to His heart. He said, *"I know your worries, your cares, and your disappointments. Leave them here with Me; I will give you rest. All is well."*

By faith, I surrendered my burdens to Him and instantly felt the weight lift from me. In the spirit, my body became limp, and He laid me down in a green pasture surrounded by beautiful flowers to rest in His glorious light.

The Banquet

As I thanked the Lord for all He had done, I saw a banquet table. Heaven said, "There is a celebration today. We are celebrating you—the children of God." The Father is always celebrating His kids.

This was a season of merriment, the season of *Shavuot*: the giving of the Law to Moses and the giving of the Holy Spirit to the sons as a comforter. It is a time to celebrate new life. A time of birth, rebirth, consecration, and dedication as the seasons change.

Heaven said, "Come feast on the fullness of all the Lord has for you.

"This is a season of escalation. Your territory in the Kingdom and on Earth is expanding and growing. Your business is expanding. Your jurisdiction as a governing, legislative, and judicial son of God is increasing. Great is He who dwells within you; and therefore, your inheritance shall be great. Your victories will increase as you overcome the battles ahead. Fight diligently in prayer. Strongholds have already fallen, and more will collapse with the shofar-blast of your shout as you move into the new season.

Holy Spirit said, *"The Father has been speaking to you. Have you been listening? Have your eyes been watching for natural signs with supernatural meaning?"*

I remembered the countless times I had seen 11:11 on the clock—times of transition—and the repeating eights on license plates, trucks, even buildings, signaling new beginnings. The Lord had been speaking; I had not been listening.

I then heard the Holy Spirit say, *"Do not be hard on yourself. Many are the pathways the righteous walk, and few are the doorways leading to destruction. Trust the Lord and His plans for your life, and all will be well. Honor Him with the first of all harvests, and abundance will continue to increase in supernatural ways."*

I then heard the Father add, *"All I have for you, My son, is in here." I saw a beautiful clam shell open, revealing a pearl. "This is a pearl of wisdom. Let wisdom guide you, for all her paths are peace and righteousness."*

The Holy Spirit continued, *"As you engage wisdom, the plans of man will appear foolish, for the counsel of the wise will be revealed to you. Seek the counsel of Heaven early and often, that your ways may be set right. Your actions will always be aligned when you seek first the Kingdom of God."*

The Long Journey

In another engagement, I heard a firm exhortation in the spirit. I knew immediately the Father was speaking as He gave me a word of knowledge for the days ahead, *"My son, today is the day of the long journey."*

As He spoke, I saw before me a long and winding road.

I heard a scripture from the book of Matthew:

> *Enter through the narrow gate; for the gate is wide and the way is broad that leads to destruction.* (Matthew 7:13-14, NASB)

"You are entering into a season of great fruitfulness," He continued. *"As you cross from pruning into growth, you will feel shifts and changes. New mantles will be given to you. New responsibilities given to you, and the desires of your heart unlocked. I am pleased with your conduct and maturation even in the face of uncommon adversity. You have been tested and tried, and you have remained steadfast. You have been victorious through the intensity."*

Two angels appeared at each side of the path, sounding shofars. Beyond them stood two men in white garments, also sounding shofars. I could see the sound waves moving forward, shifting the atmosphere.

Matthew 7:6 came to mind:

> *Do not give what is holy to the dogs; nor cast your pearls before swine, lest they trample them under their feet, and turn and tear you in pieces.* (NASB)

The Holy Spirit spoke, *"Guard your heart, rend your heart and not your garments. It is the Father who orders your steps, and He orders your tests."*

As I listened, I could see a giant red "A+" appear in the spirit. I heard the Father speak encouragement and say, *"You have done marvelously, My son."*

Suddenly, I was before the throne. Many attended Him, and the cloud of witnesses surrounded me, applauding. Jesus gazed into my eyes and said, *"Well done, My good and faithful one. Well done."*

Chapter 10
The Seven Mountains

One day, as I spent time in the secret place, I was taken into a vivid vision in which I saw a mountain rising from the ground. Surrounding it were six other mountains. I heard Heaven say, "These are your Seven Mountains of influence."

The **Mountain of Family** held authority over my family line and generations.

The **Mountain of Entertainment** represented influence over the frequency of Heaven—podcasts, creative productions, and media.

The **Mountain of Arts** held influence over *29Eleven Design & Marketing*, as well as my musical and artistic giftings.

The **Mountain of Ministry**—or Religion—carried authority over all my ministerial activities and Lighthouse Family Ministries.

The **Mountain of Education** governed books, teaching, coaching, and instruction.

The **Mountain of Finance** influenced my job, entrepreneurial work, companies, and every field the Father gave me to reap and sow in.

Finally, the **Mountain of Governmental Influence** was a place of governing as a son—intercession that reached across the Earth.

The Holy Spirit continued speaking, *"Everyone has seven mountains, just as the Earth has mountains that shape society. People have mountains of influence in the realms the Father has given them jurisdiction over. Some have more; some have fewer. The Father gives according to what His sons and daughters can steward.*

"Your mountains interconnect with each other, with your calling, and with your destiny. Though each mountain holds a specific position of influence, they work together in unity to accomplish what the Father has entrusted to you.

"Your mountains interface with the stars over the respective entities they govern; they work harmoniously with the hosts of Heaven to fulfill the mandates the Father has set for your place of authority.

"Do not neglect your mountains, for all hold relative importance in the pathways of your destiny. Claim your

throne. Call forth the blessings of the Father to be released over your places of influence, that you may experience the full manifestation of all the Father desires you to steward."

Understanding Spiritual Mountains

As I pressed in to understand more about the concepts contained in my first book, *The Ancient Pathways of Heaven*[1]*:* blueprints, destiny scrolls, trade routes, star maps, stars, and mountains, the Father further explained some intricate details of their composition to me:

- **Blueprints** are the framing and foundation of a life, business, or ministry—what the Father originally intended.
- **Destiny Scrolls** form the structure—like insulation, sheetrock, or roofing—revealing His will and the shape of destiny.
- **Trade Routes** carry resources from Heaven to Earth, like wiring and plumbing.
- **Star Maps** are points of access where Heavenly resources pass through the celestial realm and the hosts of Heaven.

These concepts relate to the time of your birth and what Heaven has placed inside you or intended for your existence. Though counterfeited by the enemy through astrology, they

---

[1] Scroll Publishers, 2024.

originated as Kingdom design. Genesis 1 reveals this through the celestial signs surrounding Jesus' birth—the star of Bethlehem being a convergence of Heavenly bodies announcing the Messiah.

The Father showed me how it relates to prayer:

- **The blueprint**—like a container in coding—the beginning and end are *"Father God"* and *"In Jesus' name, amen."*
- **The Destiny Scroll**— *"I ask You to bless Stephanie"*—represents the structure; the Father desires to bless His daughter or release His will.
- **The trade route**— *"with supernatural breakthrough"*—is the resource path.
- **The star map**—the point of access— *"in her life, business, and ministry."*

Regarding mountains, I was shown that they are Heavenly destinations—like a second home. If you do not occupy them, someone else will. Just as an abandoned vacation home may attract squatters or thieves, unoccupied spiritual mountains do the same. When you discover these intruders, you call on Heavenly authority to remove them. This process involves evicting spiritual squatters through the authority of Jesus, reclaiming your throne, your storehouses, and the places from which Christ intends you to rule and reign.

Scripture gives many examples of mountains, but two that came to mind during prayer are Matthew 17—Jesus at the Mountain of Transfiguration—and Moses at the top of Mount Sinai to receive the commandments from God. That was also a time of consecration for him, when he stood on holy ground. We all desire to be alone with the Lord, on holy ground, seeking Him in intimacy... amen?

Mountains are also frequently seen as meeting places with God in Scripture. We do not want the enemy controlling these high places or their portals. We want Heaven's armies to have control so that Kingdom resources and the things of God flow freely.

I was given one more example at this point, and it stirred my spirit. I was shown how Noah's ark landed "on the mountains of Ararat" (Genesis 8:4). All this talk of mountains in the Word pushed me further down the path of asking the question, "Father, what do You want to show me about mountains? Why are they important? How do You want me to engage them?"

Below is the prayer strategy or process of engaging Heaven's resources I was given in a Courts of Heaven Prayer paradigm

The Process (Courts of Heaven Prayer)

- In the name of Jesus, I request entrance to the Celestial Court of Heaven, appear before the Ancient of Days. I ask for Counsel & Wisdom to be present, and the Holy Spirit to guide me (this is a very holy courtroom, and you will feel a shift in the weightiness).

- As I come before You, God the Just Judge, I point my finger at the illegal activity of the enemy encroaching or squatting on my mountain, my stars, and every Heavenly place in my governance.
- I repent for not occupying my territory in the spirit and for (list any legal rights Holy Spirit reveals you need to repent for here).
- Ask the blood of Jesus to cover the legal rights and wash them away.
- Ask for the celestial angels to remove the principalities, squatters, evil entities, and bring them to the abyss.
- Ask for angels to come and cleanse the realms.
- By faith, have your spirit take the seat of authority on your throne in these heavenly structures with Jesus.

Chapter 11
Learning to Trust in Him

Learning to lean into the Father when times get tough is a rewarding spiritual discipline. Often, the biggest challenge to engaging Heaven comes from the limitations we place on ourselves. Our belief system influences our ability to receive Him as the King of Glory and Lord of all. Wounds and traumas from the past can also prevent us from fully feeling His presence or, worse yet, knowing His goodness. As you engage with this chapter, allow old hurts, mindsets, and religion to melt away and approach Heaven unhindered.

During a season of learning to trust the Father, one afternoon I lay down on my couch and tried to calm my mind. I put on some soaking worship music and pressed into the spiritual realm. Inside, I felt tired and needed to seek the Father's presence. I was weary, tired, and exhausted. As I lay there, feeling the music shift the atmosphere around me, I saw my spirit man before a well, drinking water—lapping it up like an animal who hadn't had its thirst quenched for ages.

Suddenly, the scene shifted. I saw myself walking through a residential neighborhood; overhead, dark storm clouds gathered. Suddenly, it started to rain—a torrential downpour. I could hear thunder, and I noticed I wasn't getting wet. Looking up, I saw an umbrella over my head, and Jesus was right beside me, holding it.

I could feel a deep peace, and even though a storm raged around me, I felt only serenity by His side. I noticed a man walking toward us; it was John the Baptist. John said, "The Lord is preparing His way in you. You have been called to prepare the way of the Lord; you are the restorer of breaches, the one who stands in the gap. You are a commander of the Lord's armies, one who will unleash Heaven on Earth and command forces of light to end the reign of terror and darkness that runs rampant on the Earth."

I saw lightning strike from Heaven—beautiful and terrifying. As it hit the ground, it spread along the streets and up the walls of structures. These were the lightnings of God; they looked humanoid but were more—they were elemental, the lightning bolts of God's righteousness.

Jesus's presence intensified in the natural, and I began to weep as I recognized His nearness. He spoke, *"Beloved, I see where you are weak. I know you have felt lost and confused, but these trials will pass. Feelings can be fleeting in moments of great pressure and distress, but My peace will always be your guide. When you hunger and thirst for My righteousness, you will always be sustained in Me."*

I heard the Spirit whisper, *"Come to Me, all you who are weary and burdened, and I shall give you rest."*(see Matthew 11:28)

Jesus handed me a scroll and said, *"Trust in Me. Trust the process. Do not lose hope but use your hope to free those who are bound."*

The scroll was a trust of the Father as my provider. I inquired, "May I see my trusts in Heaven?" Suddenly, I saw mountains and hills made of gold and many riches.

I heard Heaven say, "These are the lost inheritances of many generations; they are given into your hands. They are promises your ancestors missed out on, but their portion is yours."

By faith, I began to speak them into existence, reclaiming them and asking for angels to be sent to protect their delivery and ensure they were not lost or stolen.

Suddenly, I was back in the storm, but the rain had turned to gold, gemstones, and a variety of treasures falling from the sky. The clouds parted, the thunder ceased, and above me was a double rainbow. Jesus looked at me and smiled. He said, *"It's all about perspective. If you're not expecting Heaven's best, change your perspective. Trust that the Father is always God. Trust that you are blessed and destined for success. Believe for the goodness of God to manifest."*

Just as quickly as it began, the encounter was over.

Understanding Honor

In another experience, I was awakened to the understanding of the word *honor* and its meaning. As I sought guidance from Heaven on what honor truly entails, this is what I heard the Holy Spirit whisper to me, *"What does it mean to honor someone?"*

I pondered this question in my mind but didn't have an answer. After a brief pause, the Holy Spirit continued to speak, *"Honor is a form of reverence; it's a posture of humility toward others, allowing you to show appreciation, adoration, praise, value, and to hold them in high regard.*

"Honor is also a way of blessing others."

As I heard this, I saw a golden rose fall from Heaven. The dialogue continued, *"In Scripture, the Song of Solomon is a poem of honor to one's beloved. Jesus honored the disciples by washing their feet. David honored Jonathan by having Mephibosheth eat at the king's table. Rahab honored the Israelites by hiding the Jewish spies. This was done because of God; He showed mercy to Rahab as she lived in a place where no mercy was shown to her. The widow of Zarephath honored Elijah with her home and the last of her oil and flour. And in turn, Elijah honored her by crying out to God for her son to be raised from the dead and brought back to life.*

"When we honor one another, we keep the greatest commandments: to love the Lord our God with all our heart, soul, mind, and strength, and to love our neighbor as ourselves. These two commands are the epitome of the Ten Commandments given by God to Moses. God has honored us time and again—from His covenant with Abraham to His great compassion in redeeming all humanity, coming in the marred image of man as our Savior. And He will continue to honor us by bringing us into the new Heaven and new Earth on the last day, as we honor Him with our worship and adoration for all eternity.

"Jesus honored all humanity by going to the cross and dying a horrific death for our sins so that we could be free. To honor is to love; it is our opportunity to show the face of God to others and manifest Jesus to those who have been hurt or broken.

We love because God first loved us. (1 John 4:19)

Jesus taught honor to the disciples with lessons about forgiveness: how many times must we forgive? Forgiving and showing grace are acts of honor.

"When we bless those who curse us and show kindness to those who persecute us, we are honoring them and simultaneously obeying God's instruction not to avenge ourselves but to let Him heap hot coals upon the heads of opposing forces. As pride lies just below the surface of sin, honor can be found behind every act of selfless love.

"Every act of honor is a righteous trade on behalf of the Father; its fruit will be bountiful, its goodness measureless, and its impact beyond the scope of human imagination or comprehension."

Storm Catchers

In another encounter with Heaven, I was taught about standing firm during life's storms and given strategies to overcome them. As I leaned into the Holy Spirit to understand this, here is what Heaven had to say: "The storms of life will toss your ship to and fro."

As I heard Heaven say this, I could see a boat on choppy waters amid a thunderstorm, getting thrown around as the waves swelled and sloshed around it.

I heard Heaven say to commission the angels to suppress the storms. I was told there is a tool they can ask for called storm catchers. This device resembled a vase with a narrow neck and an opening at the top, similar to a bottle. It acted like a vacuum that would draw out the frequencies and energy from within a storm. The process would simply cause the storm to collapse inward or dissipate. As I watched, I saw the angels using these devices on what looked like storm clouds and tornadoes, which then seemingly just vanished. The waves stopped, and the boat remained still on the water.

The Holy Spirit spoke, *"Be at peace and be still, do not let fear and worry overwhelm you at every turn, meet opposition with overwhelming faith and recumbent peace. Let the peace of God be your greatest ally in all of your paths. The paths of life are filled with challenges and opposing forces, but the peace of God will give you a steadfast stillness that will guide you all your days."*

As I continued to process this revelation and exhortation, I was taken through a portal in Heaven that led to a room filled with people from the cloud of witnesses. I was approached by a group of individuals who seemed joyful to see me. They greeted me warmly and had gifts in hand they wanted to give me. The first people I recognized in the spirit as Elisha, Elijah, and Samuel, who imparted blessings to me. They prayed over me to receive the fullness of the prophetic mantle, to be filled with boldness, and to increase in the ability to hear and accurately convey the word of the Lord.

I was then given a set of golden gloves, which the Holy Spirit said were infused with God's healing virtue and symbolize the power of divine intervention. These biblical forefathers spoke and shared their struggles during their earthly journeys with me. They expressed that my prayers had been answered and that I was navigating through adversity, which would in turn ignite the fire within me to burn even brighter. I was reminded not to lose hope, for as they spoke, they conveyed that everything the Father allowed me to experience was ultimately for my good. I was encouraged to focus my mind on the Kingdom, because in doing so, my dreams and visions would flourish.

As the vision ended, I heard Heaven say, "Before a true prophet can fully accept their calling, essential preparation must occur. The prophet is a powerful warrior for the Lord, and those with wrongful motives can cause serious spiritual damage to others. Therefore, it is written that all whom the Father chooses must go through refinement and training in His righteousness to walk in His ways and avoid stumbling. Be still, child. Know that the Lord is God, and trust in Him."

Heaven's Nature

During this same season, as I continued to seek and learn more about trusting the Father, I was reading 2 Corinthians 11:24–28 when I heard the Holy Spirit say, *"These are the many sufferings for those who follow Christ."*

Suddenly, in the Spirit, I could see Paul. He gently grabbed my face and greeted me. He said all of Heaven was so proud of me and the work I was doing. I responded by thanking him for the encouraging words but explained that often I felt like I wasn't doing that well or even was failing.

Paul said, "That is human nature, not Heaven's nature."

Heaven overlooks even the smallest offense and celebrates every minor victory. The Father marvels at and adores all His sons—those progressing confidently and those just beginning their journey in sonship. The will of a son is mighty, unwavering, and never accepts *no* as an answer. Even if the sons stumble, fall into temptation, or falter, they get back up without a condemning spirit and turn their faces toward the Father for guidance and direction.

The sons lay down their lives for others—both those in righteousness and those in sin—because that display of love will conquer their hearts and a multitude of sin. Sons walk with authority and tear down strongholds through words and actions, living according to the Torah and demonstrating acts of love and kindness.

Jesus approached us and said, *"Walk steadfast, young one. Allow yourself to be refreshed by these words. Fasten your belt and hold tight to truth, for its light will set you free and keep you on the path of life. Don't limit yourself with fragile, self-defeating thoughts; let My life flow in and through you. In all that you do, be cheerful and take heart, for I am always by your side."*

Four Winds

Jesus said, *"There are things you are walking through in this season that are meant to grow you for your next role. The time of pressure and discomfort is over for now; it is time to return to the altar, to a place of deep and intense intercession, weeping for others and praying for their breakthrough to overtake them.*

"You shall be called a man of Glory, for the glory of God rests heavily upon you. Prophesy to the four winds of change, provision, and the dismantling of stagnation. Let the sting hills be torn down, and a deeper cultivation of intimacy begin today.

"You will be like Daniel in this season, and you will dream many dreams. You will be a leader over all the sustenance, just as Joseph was in his day, over all the land, if you continue to walk in righteousness, following the Father's commands, every jot and tittle."

Living Stones

Enoch walked up and placed a pile of white-blue stones on the table before me. They were small, and as I gazed at their beauty in wonder, I heard the Holy Spirit say, *"These are the living stones."*

These stones vibrate at the frequency of Heaven; they emanate the light of the Lord. They are the structures through which the power of God is manifested through the voices, intentions, and actions of His sons.

As I looked back at the living stones, they seemed to float off the table in front of me, one by one flying down into my abdomen. As they entered, it appeared that my body rippled like still waters when a stone is thrown into them. I instantly realized they were doing a cleansing work from the inside out.

The worries, fears, anxiety, and areas where I hadn't fully trusted or had faith were immediately brought into submission to the Word of the Lord through the reverberation of Heaven's frequencies. The Glory of the Lord was rumbling inside me, blasting away the frequencies of hell that wanted to stay rooted in my physical being.

I could see a change in my body as it became more glorified, and the areas that were once darkened by circumstances were now illuminated by the Glory of the Lord.

Chapter 12
The Father's Warning

As I entered the secret place on June 9, 2023, I saw a gathering in the Heavens. I recognized my angel Philip and wept with joy as I saw him and Jesus greeting me. As they spoke with me, I saw a great comet in the sky. The Holy Spirit said this was a harbinger of things to come. *"This is a sign of the times, a time when the Earth falls into deeper darkness—yet you and others in the Kingdom will shine with the brightness of Heavenly light. This sign, this harbinger, is a beacon of blessing to the obedient but will be as a curse to those who have embraced the lewd and corrupt ways of Satan."*

I saw what looked like meteorites or asteroid strikes happening in various countries. I heard the Father say, *"The stench of their sin stings My nostrils; the stench is as dung baking in the desert sun. But the aroma of the righteous walking in uprightness and the sweet incense of fervent prayer is pleasing.*

"My son, take heed and prepare your heart. The next four years will be a time of great turmoil and unrest upon the Earth, although My children will be spared from famine, pestilence, and sword. Yet great will be the fiery ordeals that will prepare them for the greater Glory they are being cultivated to walk in.

"You will see turmoil and upheaval in the U.S. presidential election of 2024. The evil of past seasons will try to reemerge, but this time I will expose the wicked as a floozy whose nakedness has been revealed to the world. Nations will learn of the defilement that has been covered up by distraction, and those responsible for control and manipulation will be rounded up like cattle for slaughter.

"By the end of 2030, the preparations for the third temple will be complete and in order, but My anger will burn fiery and hot on the day of its dedication against those who will place idols in the holy place as objects of their devotion.

"My people have been blinded by division, religious and political arguments—with many being correct while they themselves are trapped in error. Do not be like a hypocrite, but as one who is willing to hear My heart. Do not let the offense of or toward another cause you to stumble. The foolishness of idle arguments has brought great men to their knees and given the enemy access to their hearts. Love as I have taught you to love—love the sinner and the saint.

"Have I called you to protest your own convictions and offenses? Have I told you to hold harsh and strict judgments against those who have defiled My covenant and My Earth? Or have I yet commanded you to love your neighbor as yourself, to pray for those who curse you, bless those who oppose you, and minister the gospel to the four corners of the Earth?

"Have I not told you that you would face tribulations, that your own family would oppose you for the sake of My name? Have I not shown you the majesty and power of Heaven? Have My chosen ones strayed away from idol worshippers, sinners, and the lost, or have they gone into the cities of the lost and preached the resurrection by which all can be saved? Go and do likewise."

Political Spirit and Jezebel's Control

As I continued in prayer and engaging with Heaven, Jesus and the Father spoke to me and began to explain that all who are on the Earth are in the midst of great trials— *"a fiery ordeal."* The Father referenced Shadrach, Meshach, and Abednego (Daniel 3:19–25).

As I read the Scripture, I had a vision of the entire Earth. I saw twin snakes slithering around the circle of the Earth, coiled and squeezing all of humanity. When the two snakes came together to form a grotesque, beastly entity, I sensed it was a political spirit. I had a knowing that this same spirit was responsible for the divisions across the Earth—vaccinated versus unvaccinated, conservative versus liberal—divisions among mankind, religion, and philosophy. It caused confusion leading to backbiting and hostility.

One riding upon the serpents was a principality—Jezebel. The Lord showed me the control behind it and how it was turning all of humanity into puppets. Even in our bodies, our focus has shifted away from the Lord and into petty squabbles, where most of the Church has lost sight of the principle of loving the sinner and hating the sin. Instead, the Church has embraced an ideology of avoiding sinners, condemning the sin, and condemning those whose hearts desire to go forth and proclaim the gospel to those trapped in the deepest and darkest agendas being pushed and force-fed to all.

We have built walls that prevent us from spreading the gospel and going to the ends of the Earth to shed light into the darkness. Some worshiped the fear of compromise and embraced religious mindsets. Others embraced corruption and compromise and allowed it into the Church out of fear of being labeled bigots. Few took a righteous stand, and the ones who did were mistreated, condemned, and beaten down—even by their own.

I could see the Father weeping, His heart broken at the posture of His children—those who knew Him and those who didn't. The Holy Spirit simply said, *"Without love, there cannot be freedom."*

The Father said, *"Go forth in love, My son. I know it grieves your heart to see such defilement before you, but all things are being reconciled. In due time, all evil will be banished and abolished, and only the Kingdom of righteousness shall remain."*

Chapter 13
Crushing the Opposition

As I entered into prayer on another morning, I found myself taken into a vision walking down a white marble path to the right, with large pillars resembling columns on the left. One might see them in a Colosseum, and as I reached the end of this path, it was high above and overlooked all creation.

There was a swirl of clouds below, storm clouds with lightning; the storms of life were ransacking the peace of the land beneath. Jesus had appeared beside me as I stood watching in amazement. He said, *"My child, you're standing on the edge of consciousness, looking deep into your inner world. These storms are the storms of life—feelings of worry, anxiety, and fear that have long plagued the mind with thoughts of poverty and orphanhood. What you are witnessing is the unrestrained nature of the soul and its doubts wreaking havoc on the mind and heart's peaceful posture."*

2 Corinthians 10:5 dropped into my spirit:

> *For the weapons of our warfare are not carnal but mighty in God for pulling down strongholds, casting down arguments and every high thing that exalts itself against the knowledge of God, bringing every thought into captivity to the obedience of Christ, and being ready to punish all disobedience when your obedience is fulfilled.* (2 Corinthians 10:54-6)

As I read it, the Holy Spirit spoke these words to me, *"This is what happens when high-minded thoughts are allowed to run free. They turn the heart into a barren wasteland of anger and bitterness, and the soul becomes disobedient to the peace of God and the life of the spirit. So, by placing your soul and its cares in submission, the rule of law is laid to rest, and the flow of life from the Spirit of Christ can reign supreme in your inner being."*

As I listened and watched, Jesus placed His hand on my shoulder and spoke, *"Peace to the storms."* I saw six angels land on the platform beside us and then race down to the surface to collapse the storms that were in operation. When they returned to the platforms, the angels each had brought with them small imps. They were lies that had been trespassing on my thoughts. I stood there amazed at how such a small creature could cause such a big storm. Jesus said the lies of the enemy are destructive above all else, and the mindset they seek to distribute is death. Keep your eyes focused on me and your spirit centered on the Father's rest, and you shall not be easily deceived by such amateur tactics.

He gazed at me, remarked how much he truly loves me, and said, *"Although there is opposition, the Father's plans will succeed; the devil is running scared. When you wake up, he freaks out, wondering what you will do. You were created to be a powerful prayer warrior and to tear down strongholds."*

Then I saw a living abacus in Heaven and was told this abacus is not used like the archaic mathematical tool upon the Earth but in the heavenly realm is a keeper of eternal matters in time.

I heard the Lord say, *"There will be a shift; this is a season of blossoming."*

I saw an hourglass and was asked if I remembered the revelation of the sands of time and the hourglass. I was shown that this hourglass represented our time in the state of New York, and I could see the sands were rapidly draining from the top, with only a few grains and a thin layer left at the narrow part of the top bulb. Meanwhile, the bottom, representing Florida, was practically full.

A book flipped open, and I heard Heaven say, "This is the book of your family's destiny, your book, your destiny scroll."

The page it was opened to only had two sentences left in it. I could sense Heaven saying, "This is the end of your season in this region."

I felt as if it pertained to the end of a battle, like in a cinematic movie—the moment just before a triumphant victory.

Pushing Back the Darkness

In another heavenly encounter, as I entered the realm of the spirit, I saw a large, old-looking brown leather-bound book sitting on a table before me. The book had writing on it that said, *Destinies of the Friedman family.*

Standing near the book were two angels whom I had not previously been acquainted with. As I asked the Holy Spirit about them, I was informed that they are two of my heavenly angels operating in and from the heavenly realm. "It's nice to meet you both. What are your names?"

The first one said his name was Ramadal and the other said, "You can call me Sal." I asked them, "What do you have to tell me today?"

They responded that they had been assigned to show me what I was seeking. In this present moment, there was undue pressure pressing against me—forces moving in the supernatural realm that I had been confronting as I was shown how to war as a son. Yet they revealed that these pressures were actually components of my own soul that I was allowing to manifest. In doing so, I had been missing the glory, love, and joy the Father had been faithfully preparing for me.

I asked if they could elaborate, and they reminded me of Exodus 14:14:

> *The Lord will fight for you, and you shall hold your peace.*

I repented quickly for the fear and anxiety I had been clutching in my soul. I settled myself, stopped analyzing, leaned into the wisdom of the Holy Spirit, and fixed my attention back into the vision.

The angels opened a book as large as I was. As the pages spread, I saw what looked like a hand-drawn pop-up image of a house. A circle of light surrounded the house. Behind the light, black and purple flames reached toward it, but the light held them back.

"This fire symbolizes principalities that are trying to invade your home and steal your peace and your joy."

Dotted lines appeared, extending from the house, which sat in a valley. The lines looked like trail marks on a map leading up to a mountain summit. At the top stood another house, also surrounded by light—but this one radiated with a brilliance visible for miles, stretching to the ends of the earth. I heard Scripture rise in my spirit:

> *A city that is set on a hill cannot be hidden.... Let your light so shine before men, that they may see your good works and glorify your Father in heaven.* (Matthew 5:14, 16).

The angels then closed the book and spoke again, "Breakthrough is coming. Do not let your faith be diminished. Hold the line, advance, and push back the darkness."

As I emerged from the vision, I opened my morning devotional, *Mornings with the Holy Spirit* by Jennifer Leclaire, which confirmed the heavenly encounter I had just experienced. As I read its title, "Your Victory is Guaranteed," I marveled at how intentional the Father is to confirm the visions He gives us in the secret place.

Archangels

Early in the summer of 2023, as I was engaging Heaven in prayer, I could feel heavy opposition in the spirit. It was around the summer solstice, a period known for its heavy concentration of witchcraft, occult practices, and mysticism. As I prayed to break through what felt like resistance, I found myself in a place in the Heavenly realm that I refer to as the Court of Angels. As I entered, I saw a few Heavenly beings before me, and I inquired about strategies the sons of God can use to deal with the high-level witchcraft that surrounds the seasons marked by the solstices of the sun.

It was revealed to me that those I spoke with were Joshua and Caleb, men in white from the cloud of witnesses. They told me that we, in this court of intercession, can co-labor with Archangels and request that they be sent on assignment for the season to work with our angels.

Joshua spoke, "The Archangels are the highest class and ranking of Angels. Their capabilities span the vast spectrum of angelic assignments. They are mighty men of war with some of the most advanced resources, tactics, and know-how Heaven has to offer."

I asked if there were specific tools or resources, we could request from the Father to empower the archangels. I was told we may request the following items:

- Tools of filtering and undoing of all witchcraft
- Invisibility cloaks
- Frequency shields
- Radar bombs
- Atmosphere destroyers
- IED bombs
- Arrows of the Lord

I was then shown a destination in Heaven called the Court of the Ancient of Days. I heard the Holy Spirit instruct me to enter this place and, in prayer, request an appeal for ungodly protective coverings, celestial shielding, and the demolishing of stone structures that seek to block the prayers of the saints in the second Heaven. The Holy Spirit spoke to me, *"The prayers of the saints are powerful and effective. In times like these, praying in the Spirit for extended periods and increasing the depth of intercession will send up fiery prayers that burn through the structures created by witchcraft. All darkness can be dissolved and destroyed when armed with wisdom."*

Wars in the Heavens

In a subsequent encounter, I found myself standing on what appeared to be an aircraft carrier moving across the waters. I heard the Spirit of the Lord say to me specifically that it was an aircraft carrier—not the type we see on earth. As I looked around, instead of warplanes, I saw angels stationed nearby already. The Lord said these are the ones sent out upon the Earth to fight on behalf of His children. He mentioned that He was about to move swiftly upon the earth, impacting the lives of His sons and daughters, their marriages, and their children's lives.

This reminded me that despite the pains I am currently experiencing in the natural, weeping only lasts for a night, but joy comes in the morning.

"Angels are being sent down to destroy the plans and tactics of the forces that seek to destroy hope and joy in the hearts of the sons of God—the ones the enemy has come to kill, steal, and destroy hopes and dreams. The Lord and the righteous are fighting an all-out war to bring all His promises to pass for the good of those He loves—His sons and His daughters."

The Lord and His righteous armies are fighting a full-scale war against the forces of darkness. This is being done to ensure that all His promises are fulfilled for the good of those He loves—His sons and His daughters.

Repentance and Judgment

As I continued to seek His precious Presence, I found myself transported to the throne room, standing with my Father. Suddenly, a Heavenly gate of light opened, revealing a portal above a dark, foggy city, with a midnight purple-black sky overhead and desolate streets below. It was New York.

I heard the Lord say, *"It is turning into a haunt of jackals, the resting place of ostriches and owls."*

I started seeing many more portals open and could see San Francisco, Los Angeles, San Diego, Dallas, Oklahoma City, Denver, Bethesda, Charleston, and many other cities.

I heard the Spirit of God speak, *"The time has come for reckoning, that all who oppose shall be made to bow low. The judgments will start in thy own house—the house of God—where the workers of lawlessness and iniquity will be rooted out, and where deceptions will be exposed. My house will not be a den of devils; My house will not lust after the hearts of the earth's fornications. My people shall not be a wayward prostitute, fornicator with the sins of Jezebel and Leviathan. My name shall not be a mockery or a curse to those My Son was crucified to save. This land shall be torn apart if these people do not repent and turn from their wicked ways."*

As I heard this, I fell to my knees and began to pray and repent of the wickedness that had consumed so much of the earth. As I meditated upon this, the following Scripture resonated with me:

> *If My people who are called by My name will humble themselves, and pray and seek My face, and turn from their wicked ways, then I will hear from Heaven, and will forgive their sin and heal their land.* (2 Chronicles 7:14)

Tipping Point

As Heaven continued to hone my skills as an intercessor and increase my awareness of the authority we have as believers to push back darkness and bring forth the Kingdom,

I received the following revelation. I entered into the secret place and heard the Holy Spirit speaking, *"The enemy wants to slow you down and steamroll you, but My grace is sufficient, beloved child."*

As I heard these words from Heaven, I was sitting in my living room, having just read a devotional about the greatest revival of all time and a prophecy Smith Wigglesworth gave to Dr. Lester Sumrall in the twentieth century about walking in the power of the Holy Spirit. He said that diseases would be healed, hospitals would be emptied out, and revival would break forth upon the earth like never before.

In the spirit, I heard the Holy Spirit whisper that this mantle of revival was our portion. It was the portion of the children of God, as well as mine and my family's. At this time in our lives, the Lord had us rooted and planted in a house of worship, which had none other than Dr. Sumrall's oldest son in attendance. Frank, or Pop as we fondly called him, and his wonderful wife Karen had become like surrogate parents and grandparents to me and my family.

Heaven showed me that in the times they had prayed over us, we as a family had received the impartation of this revival fire and this mantle of miracles. I pressed into Heaven in the spirit as I heard this, and I saw the Cloud of Witnesses and angels approaching at the forefront of all my spiritual sight. I could see Smith and Dr. Sumrall, as well as Moses, Elijah, and many others who approached. They laid hands upon me in the spirit and said to me, "This is your destiny and your inheritance, and we call this mantle into full activation in your life this day."

As they laid hands on me in the spirit, I doubled over in the natural, feeling the power of God flowing through my body. Suddenly, my personal angel, Philip, handed me a small silver gift-wrapped box and a scepter. As I opened the box to see what was inside, there was a solitaire diamond ring that I put on my left hand, and the Holy Spirit said, *"This is a ring of valor, for you are a mighty man of valor."*

Then I heard the Holy Spirit say, *"Storm's coming."*

I listened intently as He expanded upon this phrase, *"The storm is coming to overthrow darkness from Heaven and onto the earth. We are at a tipping point both in the spirit and in the world; the season of justice is upon us, and the bowls of revival are being poured out upon the nations. Wrath is being poured out upon secrecy and injustice. Lies shall be exposed, and darkness overturned, for the light of the Father's Glory is refining first the body and then preparing His bride. The lost shall be saved; the days are here when old men shall see visions, and the young will dream eloquent dreams of Heaven and of My purposes for their lives. Those who know light are few; those who know darkness are many. Those walking in light are few, and those running to darkness to do evil are many. The line has been drawn in the sand, and the lot has been cast. The day of the Lord is swiftly coming like a thief in the night. Are you prepared, son of God? Is your wick trimmed? Is your lamp filled with pure oil? Be vigilant so you are not left in darkness when the lights go out."*

As I heard this, I gazed into the supernatural realm and found myself in a strategy room within Heaven. Jesus stood before me with His back to me, surrounded by others from the cloud of witnesses and many angels. On the table before us, a hologram of the entire earth was projected upward and suspended in midair.

As I looked at this hologram, I could see rockets launching in some areas and what appeared to be ground wars in others. Over these regions, I saw fierce battles taking place in the airspace—these were the armies of Heaven engaging in an assault against the principalities of darkness, trying to rule over the people of these regions.

From the depths of the earth, I saw what looked like a black hole or a portal opening, from which an ugly, serpentine creature tried to claw its way out onto the surface from below. Despite the travail and turmoil across the earth, I could sense Heaven's urgency at this moment, preparing for the White Throne Judgment and the Wedding Supper of the Lamb. The preparation process was painful, involving pruning, pressing, and being tried by fire until refined, but the final outcome was beautiful and glorious—simply beyond words.

In another vision, I saw the New Jerusalem and the Temple, the new Heavens, and the new Earth. There were trees with leaves that healed the nations, and the ethereal light of the Lord's Glory shining brightly throughout. All my spirit longed for at that moment was to gaze upon the beauty of the Lord. The circumstances did not move me to come back to earth. Still, my heart was filled with great reverence and anticipation of the Lord's return and the removal of all that was evil, so I could eternally behold His goodness, Glory, and splendor.

Jesus whispered to me, *"You are not being sifted by the enemy; God is shifting you. Your heart has been hurt, wounded, and broken, but today I trade you the broken pieces of your heart for a new heart, and I fill you with My joy and My love."*

As I heard this, I saw my heart broken into six pieces. When I handed it to Jesus, He gave me a new heart. I asked Him to invest His love and His Spirit into me, and I could feel the weeping of the Holy Spirit within me.

He spoke again, *"We are standing at the doorway of the valley of decision—a time when all must choose whether they will stand with God (and God's elect) or stand with evil and sell their souls to the Devil. There is no option to stand by idly and play the 'neutral' card; you will be casting your pearls before swine. They may be coming for the Jews now, but that means they will be coming for the heads of*

Christians next. They will come for your kids, your Bibles, your salvation—and then they will give you a choice: bow down to their idols, take a mark, or die. Today is not the day to choose to be lukewarm or cold. Tomorrow isn't guaranteed. Turn back to the one true King; in Him you will find eternal life!"

The Holy Spirit said, *"Be still and rise up, dread champion. Awaken and blaze the trail of the gospel in excellence in all you do. Pray about everything—every decision. Don't hesitate or feel compelled; instead, seek Me first and My Kingdom. All things will work out magnificently according to My divine plans."*

I was handed something like a Rubik's Cube. I was told, "This is a sequencing device. You can use it, or request and equip your angels to carry and deploy these to bring into correct sequence the divine will and blessings the Father releases to His sons. You are one such son and have the authority to bring into correct sequence and timing that which the Father desires to give the saints."

I commissioned my angels to take and use these devices as weapons, and I noticed the boxes had lights on them that fluctuated through different colors. In an instant, they were gone to carry out the Father's will, and I sat marveling at what I had just learned.

Chapter 14
Books of Destiny & Inheritance

One morning, as I entered the secret place, I was given a book called *The Book of Divine Destiny*. Along with it was a *Book of Inheritances*. As I looked ahead in the Spirit, I saw myself walking on a glowing path. Beside the path, portals of light opened, and out of them stepped individuals who resided in Heaven.

I saw Joseph and Daniel step out of the portals and walk toward me. The path opened into a valley. I was on top of a foothill, looking over many who were farming the land, tilling the soil, sowing seeds, and herding livestock. It was beautiful—reminiscent of the Great Plains region of America during the 1800s. The grass was lush and full; the wind was warm and comforting; the air was clean and crisp.

I saw the wholeness of families and their structures. Children laughed and played, walking in identity and wisdom. They were humble and obedient to their parents. Marriages were beautiful, blossoming with love, adoration, and respect. There was no fighting, no divorce, no berating of children, and no confusion. There was a purity—a love and adoration for the things of God. Although their tools and methods seemed primitive compared to today, their hearts for God were radiant and fervent.

Children sat around their mothers, listening to the reading of the Word, participating and asking questions. Fathers prayed over their families and over the seeds being sown into the soil. Time sped up, and I saw the seeds sprout and grow into tall, hearty plants. As this unfolded, I gained insight into how the Father felt when He created the world.

> *Then God said, 'Let the earth bring forth grass, the herb that yields seed, and the fruit tree that yields fruit according to its kind, whose seed is in itself, on the earth'; and it was so. And the earth brought forth grass, the herb that yields seed according to its kind, and the tree that yields fruit, whose seed is in itself according to its kind. And God saw that it was good.* (Genesis 1:11-12)

As I marveled at the scene, I felt the goodness of God. This was inheritance—*to be fruitful and multiply.* For the children to flourish in these things. This was destiny as the Father intended: wholeness and blessing.

Suddenly the scene sped forward, as though I were transported into the future. I saw laziness and perversity invade people's minds. The Earth became barren and stopped yielding fruit. Marriages dissolved, replaced by lies of pleasure without promise and intimacy without covenant. As *fatherhood* vanished from the home, suicide, divorce, abomination, and sexual immorality tempted humanity, turning God's good creation into debauchery. War, sickness, rebellion, and widespread chaos overtook the Earth.

This was a timeline in which mankind chose to abandon their God-given destiny. They forsook their inheritances, allowed the thief to steal their good things, and lusted after what was profane.

A glowing light descended from Heaven in front of me. It was the brightest thing in the entire scene, while everything else seemed swallowed in darkness. It was Jesus.

"This is the cost the world will pay for choosing to do things its own way."

I felt sickened and grieved at how easily humanity could turn away from God and open the door to such suffering. Jesus gazed at me with a loving smile and tear-filled eyes. My spirit received His instruction, *"Dedicate your children to God, and point them in the way they should go, and the values they learn from you will remain with them for life."* (see Proverbs 22:6)

I knew that through obedience to this instruction, we—and the body of Christ—could embrace our God-appointed destiny and inheritance so that it would not be lost or stolen.

Our children and our children's children are that inheritance. By amplifying the anointing upon their lives and demonstrating the importance of loving God and one another, we ensure revival and preserve the seed so precious to the Father.

As I looked back toward what had been darkness, it was transformed by the light of His glory. I knew we were entering an age of restoration and redemption—but only if we chose to return to the Lord, to seek Him in intimacy, so we could find the good way and walk in it.

Destined for Victory

During the spring of 2022, as I was spending time in the secret place, Jesus met me in a place that looked like a heavenly business complex. From the outside, it appeared as a glorious office structure with unique glass walls, waterfalls, and lush trees in the atrium. It bustled with angels and saints engaged in the Father's business.

Jesus looked at me with deep affection. This was a season of hardship and adversity in the natural—one I could endure only by seeking Him daily for rest and strength. He said, *"Even though there is opposition, the Father's plans will succeed. The devil is running scared, and when you wake up, he panics, wondering what you will do. You were created to be a powerful prayer warrior and to tear down strongholds."*

Then I saw a living abacus. I was told that, unlike the mathematical tool on earth, this abacus in the heavenly realm is a keeper of eternal matters in time. I heard the Lord say, *"There will be a shift; this is a season of blossoming."*

I saw an hourglass. I was asked if I remembered the revelation of the sands of time. This hourglass represented our time in New York. The sands were rapidly draining from the top, with only a few grains left. Meanwhile, the lower bulb—Florida—was nearly full.

A book flipped open before me, and I heard Heaven say, "This is the book of your family's destiny—your book, your destiny scroll."

The page it opened to had only two sentences remaining. I sensed it pertained to the end of a battle—like the moment in a film just before a triumphant victory.

Destroyer of Destinies

At another time, as I sat with the Lord and asked what was on His heart, I heard Him speak, *"The enemy is attempting to destroy destinies. That is why suicide and drug overdose is increasing. The army the Lord is raising up—many whom others might overlook or question—are the targets. They carry high callings and will experience glorious salvation and testimonies.*

"Look at your own life and destiny. You were one the enemy sought to deceive through drug use, attempting to deliver the same death blow. But you cried out to the Lord, and He delivered you, placing you on the path of your destiny. And what a wonderful destiny it is.

"All God's children are called to know Him and to experience His wonder in their assignments. This infuriates the enemy and drives him to increase his attacks—but darkness will not prevail against His higher glory!

"Abortion is not the devil's only tactic to abort destinies. Be wise to this and help others overcome by the blood of the Lamb. The enemy is targeting families—especially kingdom marriages—attempting to disrupt those with the highest callings who walk in the authority given in Christ Jesus.

"There is an assault aimed at derailing saints from their destinies, distracting them with natural storms and events to weary them and make them feel depressed. The leviathan spirit is behind this. Its goal is to divide those who will raise up future generations of kingdom builders, financiers, and kingdom children.

"This will not last. It is a failed attempt by a fallen and defeated foe. These attacks can only distract those who allow these lies to tower over them like giants. In reality, when you stand in Christ, they are insignificant gnats.

"Stand in your authority and take up your sword against these attacks—they are already thwarted and defeated. Do not be misled by the flesh or the soul. Trust in God and be led by the Spirit, and you will see the victory."

Chapter 15
Breakthrough to Breakthrough

During a season of laboring in prayer for breakthrough in my region and business, I was brought back into Heaven's business complex. As I stepped into the building in this vision, I found myself inside a conference room. Enoch, Moses, and Abraham were already seated there, along with angels and other men and women in white who were assigned to my affairs. Jesus sat at the head of the conference table.

I noticed Gloria—a woman in white who carries manuscripts. One scroll hovered above her head while four others were tucked in her arms. She extended her hand and gave me a scroll, and Jesus said, *"Open the scroll. Break the seal; you have been found worthy."*

As I opened it, the scroll initially appeared to be a blueprint—filled with designs, dimensions, and instructions. But then I noticed notations written within it. The first read:

Declarations of Faith

Followed by:

Prayers That Bring Breakthrough

I asked Heaven what these things meant, and I was told they were the recipe for success in all things. Enoch began to speak, "This is a two-step process by which the substance of faith can be released into the earth to fulfill the plans of Heaven—the plans the Father has placed within you."

This was the manifestation of His words in Jeremiah 29:11:

> *For I know the thoughts that I think toward you, says the Lord, thoughts of peace and not of evil, to give you a future and a hope.*

Abraham then spoke, "Today, you embark on a new journey. As you step forward, the blessings of the Lord shall overtake you to a greater degree because of your obedience as a son and your desire to seek Him—even in adversity.

"Your struggles have not gone unnoticed. Your hardships have not been overlooked. The process you have endured has not been dismissed. You have been tested and found worthy to walk in a greater level of anointing.

"In this place, you will teach, counsel, minister, and disciple. You will bring others into a greater knowledge of the Kingdom dynamics available to them so they may hear from

Heaven, seek God's face, and know the plans He has for their lives."

Moses spoke next, "This is a season of deliverance for the oppressed. In you, others see the light of hope. In your words, they find comfort and the courage to believe again—that they can be set free.

"As you go forth to speak, many will listen; many will glean from your journey. Hearts that have grown cold toward prayer and toward believing in God will reignite, and faith will be stirred once more. They will turn back to the God of Abraham, Isaac, and Jacob."

I asked the Lord, "What are my next steps?"

He said, *"Be still to receive. Keep your heart postured to hear from Heaven. Walk with Him. Do as He does. Do not be distracted by the things that would pull you off course."*

I heard Heaven say, "This is the decade of breakthrough..." (referring to my forties).

I began weeping. I saw myself at the feet of Jesus, asking why I had been so fortunate to live when others I had grown up with had died or fallen into chaos.

The Holy Spirit said, *"The journey of those called to prophetic ministry is never easy. The path is riddled with brokenness, but the rewards harvested along the way are beyond compare.*

"What you see, you will find. What you open will be redeemed as long as the Lord remains at the center of your gaze. Lock eyes with Jesus. You are on the threshing floor. This threshing will not break you—it will birth something wonderful, lasting, and necessary."

Crown & Mantle of Glory

As I pressed in, I heard the Father say, *"I am giving you a crown of Glory."*

He handed it to me. Overwhelmed, I asked why. I felt myself choking up.

He said I deserved it—that it was a symbol of His Glory resting upon me because I could be trusted. Then He placed a mantle of Glory on my shoulders and said this would increase the manifestation of His Glory in my life—that if I stepped into revival, it would break out simply because of His Presence resting upon me.

He said I was receiving these because I had triumphed through tests and could be trusted with greater things—because He knew my heart and my willingness to listen and yield to Him.

He continued, *"I want you to stop waiting for a word from others. Seek Me, and I will show you what you need to know. Stop waiting for others to pray over you, for it is I who will lay hands on you and cover you in prayer. I will shield you from the wounded souls who hurt and judge. I will continue to grow and expand you beyond your limits."*

Convergence

On the morning of Saturday, November 25, 2023, I stepped into Heaven feeling weary. It was the weekend after Thanksgiving, and although I had taken a vacation in nature, the time away felt busier than my workweek. My spirit felt dry and in need of refreshing.

As I entered, I walked through two wide-open golden doors with radiant white light pouring down the corridor. The doors were so massive I felt like an ant stepping through the frame.

Farther down the hallway, I noticed five pathways converging at a single point. This was where pathways of destiny met. Angels rushed about with books and scrolls—filing them, opening them, and bringing them to those seeking God's wisdom. Though it resembled a library, I sensed it was part of the Court of Destiny.

A woman in white named Millie approached. Seeing my curious expression, she asked if I needed help. I asked where we were. Millie said, "We are in the Hall of Destiny. This is the repository of all archives of destiny for all time. It is accessed through prayer by those seeking the Father's will."

As she spoke, these verses stirred in my spirit:

Don't let worry enter your life... your heavenly Father knows your every need... As you passionately seek His Kingdom above all else, He will supply your needs. (Luke 12:29–31)

When I read the passage, I trembled as the anointing of the Holy Spirit washed over me. The previous season had required constant laboring, and I often wondered when the harvest would come. This was a reminder to trust God's timing rather than my own understanding.

As we walked, I saw glimpses of biblical moments—how God repeatedly turned dire circumstances into good. Then we entered another corridor, and what I saw took my breath away.

I saw the One seated on the throne holding a scroll sealed with seven seals. A mighty angel proclaimed, "Who is worthy to open the scroll and break its seals?"

But no one was found worthy, and I felt the grief John described in Revelation. Then an elder declared, "Stop weeping. Look! The Lion of the tribe of Judah... He is worthy." (see Revelation 5:1–5)

Millie explained that understanding destiny requires recognizing the worthiness of the call—and the price Jesus paid. Human ideas lead to poverty and weakness, but God's plans lead to excellence, provision, and strength. When we rely on our own ideas, we become stretched thin by the world, but when we depend on Him, He leads us surely.

Technologies of Heaven

In another encounter, the Holy Spirit addressed my belief systems and told me that much of modern science is flawed or incomplete. I recalled reading about the discovery of "white holes" in the galaxy when one of my angels began speaking.

They explained that what astronomers call white holes and black holes are actually Heavenly technologies—entry and exit points connected by wormholes. Like mirrors of each other, they function as interdimensional passageways.

The Holy Spirit revealed these were *portals*—the same kind opened through Spirit-led prayer, through which angels and Heavenly armies travel on assignment. He also revealed that hell had corrupted aspects of this technology for evil purposes.

As prayer warriors, we have authority to destroy demonic portals with our spoken word and to live under the open Heaven the Father intends for us.

Following Him Night & Day

One evening, I had a vision of walking down a grassy slope toward a lake. Massive waterfalls cascaded on either side. Across the water stretched a path of golden lily pads. As I crossed them, a staircase appeared with seven images of Jesus—each a color of the rainbow. They merged into one, revealing the seven Spirits of the Holy Spirit.

Before the throne of the Most High, I heard, *"Bow down, son of man."*

I fell on my face in the spirit. Revelation flowed, *"Be still and know what lies ahead is the next leg of your journey.*

"Do you know why I'm sending you to Florida? There's a war coming."

When I asked if He meant in the supernatural realm, He answered, *"Yes. What you have fought through here will be used to encourage and inspire many who have never faced such oppression or fear."*

Then the Scripture came to mind:

> *Call to Me, and I will answer you, and show you great and mighty things.* (Jeremiah 33:3)

As I prayed, I heard a voice I initially assumed was my angel, Phillip. But the speaker identified himself as Stewart—

a man in white who had been assigned to assist me. He began explaining the importance of rest and Sabbath, even in the midst of fatherhood. In his hand, he carried a vial labeled *the oil of rest.*

Stewart described my calling as similar to Timothy's or Jeremiah's—young but set apart. He mentioned that the reason I was drawn to young, empowered voices like Jerame Nelson was because of a similar anointing. Those who influenced that minister—Bobby Conner, David Herzog, Ruth Heflin, Cindy Jacobs—were part of that lineage.

I reflected on my connections within the family of God and sensed I was being positioned among those whose hearts burned for the fullness of our inheritance.

I then asked God about the roots of the attacks sent against me. I saw a field beneath swirling gray clouds—storm clouds with no rain. Burned tree roots surrounded me in a circle, still smoldering with smoke rising from them. It reminded me of Elijah calling down fire from Heaven.

As I watched, the attacks were consumed. I stepped forward, free from what once held me back.

In the spirit, I then saw fiery angels wreathed in brilliant flames. Lightning—green and yellow—shot out from the fire. When I asked the Holy Spirit about the green flame, He said that although on earth green often symbolizes envy or greed, in Heaven it represents growth, expansion, enlightenment, and maturity.

I saw my wife beside me with a green flame above her head—like cloven tongues of fire. A voice from Heaven said, "This is the flame of growth."

It marked her spiritual maturity and the flourishing of her journey. As she read a book, the flame brightened—changing from yellow to red, then blue, then green again—colors reflecting the Holy Spirit's nourishment in her heart. It was the fertile soil of a life prepared, planted, and watered by Him.

Chapter 16
On Earth As It Is In Heaven

As we embrace our sonship and recognize that the same miracle-working power Jesus carried resides within us, we are drawn into deeper intimacy and into the ability to see visions from Heaven. One morning, while meditating on the Word, I was taken into a vision in which I saw a radiant DNA helix glowing with golden light. It streamed down through a portal directly from Heaven. As I marveled, I heard the Holy Spirit say, *"This is being imparted into you—to transform your DNA into that of the Father. His plan and purpose are being downloaded into your being."*

As He spoke, I felt the Glory of God settle upon me in the natural. Suddenly, I saw waterfalls and rivers of water flowing down limestone walls. Streams emerged from the base of the wall—streams of refreshing, revelation, knowledge, and wisdom. At the top of the waterfall, I saw the Father Himself pouring out these waters upon His body.

The streams flowed into a great reservoir filled with the wisdom of Heaven. Beneath the reservoir was a spigot, from which droplets fell toward the earth. Angels received these droplets—carrying the Father's thoughts—and delivered them to the saints in various places.

Heaven's Legislative Table

In another vision, I saw Jesus seated high and lifted up at the head of a long table. Saints sat around Him, including some I recognized from the body I am established in. Each held a scepter in one hand and a shepherd's staff in the other. They wore fine white robes with golden trim and mantles of white with purple velvet inlays. Behind them stood angels and men and women in white linen, along with multitudes.

These were legislating the government of God upon the earth. Their physical vessels were stationed in earthly territories, but from Heaven they were releasing justice into those regions. At the center of the table lay a parchment with a quill writing upon it by itself. As the quill moved, new lines appeared—Heaven's mandates for the coming season.

Suddenly, a massive angel appeared and blew a long shofar. The blast thundered through the heavens. I heard Heaven declare, "The enemy's forces that have torn, destroyed, plundered, and stolen the rightful inheritances from the children of God shall be overthrown."

As the shofar sounded, platoons of angels armed with battle axes, maces, flails, and weapons of war descended to the earth. They came to overthrow thrones, principalities, and powers that had fraudulently placed themselves over God's people.

In the blink of an eye, I saw governments transformed. Leaders awoke from demonic trances. From a global vantage point, I saw hundreds of thousands fall prostrate, crying, "Holy is the Lamb of God! Holy is the Lord our God!"

Then I saw the throne of God descend into what looked like a city of limestone in Jerusalem, where He sat to rule and reign forever. I was left stunned by the scale of this revelation.

Kingdom Life, Kingdom Marriages

At another time, as I interceded for Kingdom marriages—especially my own—the Lord was teaching me how to love my wife as Christ loves the Church. I was drawn to John 10:10:

> *The thief does not come except to steal, and to kill, and to destroy. I have come that they may have life, and that they may have it more abundantly.*

As I meditated on this, the Holy Spirit began showing me couples from church who served in unity. He said, *"All of these Kingdom marriages are truly blessed, as is yours. This will be you and your honey one day. The adversity you faced is not uncommon. None of what you have experienced is outside the path of Kingdom marriages."*

He continued, *"This is a season of revival and harvest for you and your wife. Obstacles from the last season will not prevent you from stepping into fullness. This is your comeback season. Your wife's comeback season is restarting. Refreshing is coming. Great and amazing things will be revealed to you, and I will be in the midst—healing, protecting, guiding you and your beautiful family. In Jesus, you have freedom."*

Revolutionary Angels

As I listened, I entered another vision. I saw angels standing in formation, beating war drums. They wore red coats with golden trim, reminiscent of the Revolutionary War era. A voice from Heaven announced, "A revolution is coming."

The angels marched to the edge of a cloud and dove downward to their assignments. Another voice declared, "A revolution is coming—bringing newness, refreshing, and revival of things long forgotten."

Then I saw rainbow-colored waves of Glory sweeping across the earth. The Holy Spirit said, *"They carry the vibrations and frequencies of Heaven. Watch and behold the new thing the Lord is bringing."*

Blueprint from the Cloud of Witnesses

In yet another vision, I stood in a snow-covered field sparkling like diamonds. Rainbows danced across the ice-bright surface as angels flew to their assignments. A man named Richard, from the Cloud of Witnesses, approached me. He shared about his life on earth and said that people in his day feared darkness more deeply and avoided it—even to their own compromise.

He said that is changing.

Richard handed me a blue scroll. When I broke the ring and unrolled it, I saw a map, blueprint, and strategy—outlining a ministry I would one day build. But for now, the foundation was still being formed. He warned, "If the foundation is built correctly, it will be rock-solid. But do not rush it. If it is not laid properly in its time, it will crumble."

Chapter 17
He Calls the Qualified and Qualifies the Called

As I entered Heaven, I saw Daphne—an angel of mine—who appeared in the form of a winged horse. She told me she had something to show me, so I climbed onto her back. As we rode, Jesus appeared beside us. Suddenly, in the Spirit, I was shown the valley of Ben-Hinnom. I later learned this is Gehenna—"hell on the Earth" in Hebrew. The nations were gathered there as though preparing for war against the Lamb.

I noticed hot-air balloons rising above the valley and asked the Lord their meaning. As they ascended, I heard Him say, *"I gaze upon My children from the highest heavens, and I have seen much. The provocations on Earth against Heaven are great."*

In the next moment, I found myself in what resembled the temple in Jerusalem. White sandstone walls and floors gleamed, accented with gold inlays and multicolored gemstones. A man with a white beard, dressed in priestly white garments, approached the altar holding a bowl of incense.

"These are the prayers of the holy ones crying out for revival and redemption on the Earth."

I then saw a church in Jerusalem called the Church of the Holy Specular. Before my eyes, the church collapsed into rubble. From its ruins, something like a small mountain began to rise—and it didn't stop. It grew taller and taller until it overshadowed the whole Earth. I sensed a powerful religious stronghold, ancient and deeply corrupt, being revealed.

Suddenly everything fell silent. Two lightning bolts—one brilliant white, the other golden yellow—twisted together in the sky and struck the mountain's peak. The sound cracked like thunder. The mountain split cleanly in two, both sides falling away. When the dust settled, Yeshua was standing where the lightning had struck.

The Lord spoke, *"Just as Samuel anointed and removed leaders, this is your mandate as a kingmaker prophet: build up and tear down."*

Then the following scripture entered my spirit:

See, today I have appointed you over nations and over kingdoms: to uproot and to tear down, to

destroy and to overthrow, to build and to plant.
(Jeremiah 1:10, TLV)

The presence of Heaven intensified, and I soon found myself standing before the Cloud of Witnesses. Several prophets approached—Jehu and Azariah among them. I recognized them from Scripture. When I introduced myself, Azariah looked at me with surprise and said Heaven had been watching me, and that I was the Father's chosen one for this time and season.

I saw Samuel, Elisha, Obed, Obadiah, and Isaiah. I heard the name Ahaz, and as I later researched him, I was reminded of the prophetic persecution of his day—how evil rose when the prophetic voice was ignored.

Azariah explained that a prophet's role is simply to speak when God commands—not to control the outcome. A prophet must also repent and intercede for those who refuse the message, standing between Heaven and the Earth on their behalf.

Ezekiel 22:30 came to mind—God looking for someone to stand in the gap. The prophets spoke in one voice, urging me to be that one. Their words reminded me of something Cindy Jacobs once said: psychics aren't ashamed to say they're psychic, and she isn't ashamed to say she's a prophet. Then I heard the Lord tell me to stop being afraid of what He created me to be.

The Power of Fasting & Prayer

During a season of fasting, I entered the secret place and was taken into an encounter that revealed the power released when fasting becomes a way of life. As I sought the Holy Spirit about the purpose of this fast and what He wanted me to focus my prayers on, I heard Him speak to me, *"My son, you must understand something very important about prayer and fasting—especially as a prophet. Fasting sets you apart. It purifies your vessel when you lay something down to honor Me. It strengthens you spiritually and releases great power from Heaven to aid the sons of God in spiritual warfare and heavenly battles. When you pray in the Spirit while fasting, it releases tremendous power and fuels the raging fire of My movement through those who practice this discipline. Mountains will be moved. Embrace this more and more. Set aside time to seek Me while you fast—pray, pursue intimacy with the Father, and press into Heaven. You will witness the explosive power of God manifest as never before."*

Declaring the Word of Heaven

At another time during my morning commute to work, I was given a vision in which I saw myself walking up a marble staircase and through a door. I was greeted by the Lord, who explained that just as I had interceded for friends who were sick last night, He wants me to intercede continually. He told me to pray for the nation. As I looked up in the natural, I saw dark storm clouds in the sky.

The Lord said that darkness covers the land. Immediately, in the Spirit, I was with the Lord, and we were looking at Washington D.C., standing by the Washington Monument. I could see a crack in the monument, and He told me to make declarations over the nation. The first declaration was for the powers on high to fall and be brought low, that all opposition to the Lord be destroyed. The second declaration was for lightning of the Lord to strike at the heart of the capital, and for all those operating wickedness and darkness, stubborn in their hearts and bent on destroying and harming God's children, to be removed and judged. Suddenly, I saw very large hammers being dragged across the National Mall, held by extremely large angels.

I asked the Lord about the angels and the hammers; He said they were for destroying the idols of the land and those not of God. I was told these angels are called "Haberdasher angels," and their usual task is to temper the gold in Heaven and craft crowns for the saints. It's a sacred and magnificent role, but today they have a new assignment: preparing the Earth for the Lord's return, that He would be enthroned upon it, and that all His children would be redeemed. Then I noticed another group of angels—smaller in size, like fiery balls—flitting, flying, and darting in all directions. These angels were sent to go into the hearts of mankind, to reawaken those in the Body of Christ, to reignite the fervor and passion for the Lord, and to burn away the yokes of slavery and wickedness placed by religion and false doctrines.

The Lord told me, *"This is a new season, and a new kind of revival will break out—not in small pockets but in large crowds—as the Spirit of the Lord is now moving across the Earth. The night of chaos is over, and the dawn of a new day—His love and fierce retribution against those who have harmed His children—is coming."*

Suddenly, I saw from a different perspective: I could see government buildings in the capitals of each U.S. state. I saw armies of angels surrounding them, on similar missions, shaking off everything profane to the Lord and restoring what is good in His eyes. Amid these angels, I noticed others blowing trumpets and shofars, sounding the alarm that the Day of the Lord is soon to come.

As I stepped out of the encounter, I looked up and out my window. In that moment I saw a truck that said "Old Dominion," with the slogan "Helping the World Keep Promises." The Holy Spirit reminded me that, in this world and our country, the USA was initially founded on biblical principles. He then placed this scripture on my heart.

> *Then to Him was given dominion and glory and a kingdom, That all peoples, nations, and languages should serve Him. His dominion is an everlasting*

dominion, Which shall not pass away, And His kingdom the one Which shall not be destroyed. (Daniel 7:14)

UNPREPARED!

One spring morning in April of 2024, I sat alone with the Lord, preparing for a house church meeting we were to have at our home. Deep inside, a new hunger for the miraculous and the fire of God was stirring within me. As I read the Word, I entered into a vision in which I saw myself walking behind a woman dressed in a wedding gown. I was following the train of her gown dragging behind her. As I walked I noticed billions of people surrounding me; many sat to the right and left of the aisle. The rows of seats stretched so far that I could see no end to them. As I followed this bride down the aisle toward the altar, I saw a chuppah (wedding canopy used in Jewish weddings) overhead, where the groom stood. To the left and behind, there was a long table with many chairs set up for a grand celebration, the wedding feast. When the bride reached the altar, I saw the groom's face; it was Jesus. He smiled at her with radiance and admiration, took her hands, and lifted her veil to look upon her beauty. As he did, I began to focus on the bride's face, wondering what kind of face the bride of Christ might have. What I saw next stopped me cold.

Three snakes' heads emerged from the bride's neck: one yellow, one dark green, and the third brown. Jesus said, *"My bride is unprepared,"* and with authority, the snake heads split from her body and slithered down to the Earth. The bride fell back and sat at the altar, weeping, for it was her moment, yet she missed the chance to prepare for the groom's arrival.

The snakes that fell to the Earth slithered about, stirring up wars, rivalries, gossip, and slander wherever they went. They entered the ears and left through the mouths of both the elect and the common people. In their minds, they laid eggs that hatched into fruitless myths and lies, and their offspring produced more hatchlings, until even those waiting for the day of the Lord became lukewarm and cold. They grew accustomed to the darkness of perversity that had invaded the hearts of those who were once pure and blameless before God. They had fallen into deception and rebellion. I heard the scripture Jude 1:11:

> *Woe to them! For they have gone in the way of Cain, have run greedily in the error of Balaam for profit, and perished in the rebellion of Korah.*

Then came a lion who roared across the Earth, and in the roar was heard a frequency that defeated the serpents. The frequency of the roar was deafening, and those who heard it were freed from lies and clouded hearts. An angel appeared and interpreted the roar; he courageously spoke over the bride and said, "It is time to come home. Return, return, oh Zion, for the hour of redemption draws near."

With the blast of a shofar, a whirlwind swept over the planet, and all who were well prepared were brought back to the altar.

The Warriors Hammer

During Hanukkah, while I was praying, I experienced a profound revelatory encounter. I saw a table that had been prepared. It was covered with a white, glowing tablecloth. On top of the table was a golden menorah. As I looked at the table, I saw communion elements—wine and bread—seated around it, where others who are already in the heavenly realm were gathered. I noticed John (the beloved), Abraham, Moses, David, and many others standing near Jesus. I also observed a group of angels, tall, strong, and relaxed in posture. I had an inner awareness and knowing that this was Michael, the archangel, accompanied by six others of the same rank.

A man was brought before Jesus and came to join us at the table. His appearance was strong and mighty, a man of great strength, a warrior. He was introduced to me as Judah Maccabee, the leader of the Maccabean revolt against occupying powers, which is at the heart of the Hanukkah story, the feast of dedication. As I sat with those at the table, my angels gathered around me. Each of us was given a warrior's hammer. They looked much like sledgehammers.

The Holy Spirit said these hammers are significant for the season you are walking into. It is a season of breaking down walls and old ideologies that cannot go with you into this next phase of growth and development. It's demolition time—time to bring down the things that do not submit to the Lord and rebuild the altar of the Lord. Rededicate your temple to the Lord of Hosts, come back to the threshing floor, humbling yourself in His presence, and receive the Father's wisdom, His goodness, His purpose, and His plan for your destiny.

This season is a time to leave behind the old and embrace the new. New gifts will begin to form, increasing the anointing already upon your life. You shall walk in a manner worthy of the King you serve. You are called friends—the friends of God. Although the sons of God are in this season, it is your duty to listen and obey, keeping your face steadfastly fixed on the gaze of Jesus, the beauty of Heaven. Listen intently to all that is spoken and act upon it in due time. The revelation given to you in this season will be carried out swiftly and with precision.

He said, *"Jesus does not want His friends to walk with a mindset of lack. It is not His will for His friends or His sons to walk in the identities created by false realities, deception, or religion. You are no longer an orphan; you are a son, and a son knows his value in the King. Ensure that at the deepest levels of your being, all of your creation understands the weight of the debt paid upon the cross—that you may live in such a time as this and be among those gathered into the sheepfold.*

"You are living in the days of the culmination of all things. The times until the end of the age are short. Do not be deceived or misled into thinking that the return of the Messiah is not yet near, for the groundwork is being laid, and the foundations of the Earth are being shaken. All nations are rising up against the elect of God. Soon, all shall be gathered to the valley of Jehovah, where judgment and triumph will take place. Yield to the work of the Holy Spirit—flow in your life through pruning and crushing—to birth a new level of intimacy with the Father. For all who are called friends of the Father must be cleansed and purified to enter into His glorious presence. Be washed in the blood of the Lamb and renew your mind.

"Do not bathe in the criticism and judgment of self-blame and shame. Do not harp on regret or self-resentment but proclaim the day of freedom and liberty to the captive. That is your soul. Put down the baggage that weighs you down, and take up His burden, for His burden is easy and His yoke is light. And press on toward the high calling that you have been called into—the King, priest over your generations, the Melchizedek (High Priest over your family), the servant of the Most High who dwells in the lowest place of highest praise.

Let the oil being birthed in you allow you to glow brightly and be poured out upon all those around you." The encounter ended with this, and I was left sitting, pondering this revelation as the candles before me blazed brightly like the pillar of fire that gave the children of Israel light in the darkest night of their wilderness.

Description

In *Cloud by Day, Fire by Night*, Jeremy invites you on a transformational journey into the unseen dimensions of God. Through vivid encounters with the Father, the Son, the Holy Spirit, and the cloud of witnesses, the realms of Heaven open with revelation that reshapes how you see creation, purpose, and identity.

This book is more than teaching—it is a blueprint for learning to lead by following the movements of the Spirit. As you engage Heaven, you'll discover how to step into the fullness of the plans and purposes God has written over your life.

A paradigm shift .
A quantum leap forward.
A doorway into divine understanding hidden within Scripture.

What God conceals in glory, He invites His sons and daughters to seek and find.

Are you ready to step into the mystery?

About the Author

Jeremy Friedman is a prophetic teacher, evangelist, intercessor, and entrepreneur with a unique apostolic grace. His life testimony is a powerful example of God's saving power, and through his journey to faith, he has helped many others understand the heart of the Father. Jeremy's prophetic gifting enables him to perceive the world in ways that often go unnoticed, allowing him to offer deeper insights into spiritual matters.

Daily, he seeks the Lord with his whole heart, longing to receive revelation from Heaven to help build God's Kingdom on Earth. As a Jewish believer in Yeshua, Jeremy has a passion to serve as a bridge between all nations, helping people understand that they are grafted into the rich Jewish heritage of the Bible through our Messiah.

Currently Jeremy and his wife Joelene are the founders of Lighthouse Family Ministries and Lead Apostles for Crown Ecclesia, coaches for Heaven Down™ Business, and a part of the LifeSpring International Ministries team. Jeremy has a desire to show others the pathways to freedom that he himself has been brought through in deliverance ministry. He is a devoted husband and Father to five beautiful children who truly desires to see them walk in their callings and teach their generations to rise and build the Kingdom of Heaven.

Published by:

A division of LifeSpring Publishing
www.scrollpublishers.com

Has God spoken to you about writing a book?
Let us help you!

www.ingramcontent.com/pod-product-compliance
Lightning Source LLC
LaVergne TN
LVHW090940080826
845145LV00003B/822

* 9 7 8 1 9 6 2 8 0 8 3 0 9 *